The Complete Guide To

Investing In

Short-Term

Trading

How to Earn High Rates
of Returns Safely

THE COMPLETE GUIDE TO INVESTING IN SHORT-TERM TRADING: HOW TO EARN HIGH RATES OF RETURNS SAFELY

ISBN-13: 978-1-60138-002-9   ISBN-10: 1-60138-002-X

Library of Congress Cataloging-in-Publication Data

Northcott, Alan, 1951-
  The complete guide to investing in short-term trading : how to earn high rates of return safely / by Alan Northcott.
     p. cm.
  Includes bibliographical references and index.
  ISBN-13: 978-1-60138-002-9 (alk. paper)
  ISBN-10: 1-60138-002-X (alk. paper)
  1. Speculation. 2. Rate of return. 3. Stocks. 4. Stock price forecasting. I. Title.

  HG6041.N67 2008
  332.64'5--dc22
                              2007052999

INTERIOR DESIGN: Vickie Taylor • vtaylor@atlantic-pub.com
PROOFREADER: Cathy Bernardy • bernardyjones@gmail.com

Printed in the United States

Printed on Recycled Paper

We recently lost our beloved pet "Bear," who was not only our best and dearest friend but also the "Vice President of Sunshine" here at Atlantic Publishing. He did not receive a salary but worked tirelessly 24 hours a day to please his parents. Bear was a rescue dog that turned around and showered me, my wife Sherri, his grandparents Jean, Bob, and Nancy and every person and animal he met (maybe not rabbits) with friendship and love. He made many people smile every day.

We wanted you to know that a portion of the profits of this book will be donated to The Humane Society of the United States.

— *Douglas & Sherri Brown*

THE HUMANE SOCIETY
OF THE UNITED STATES ©

The human-animal bond is as old as human history. We cherish our animal companions for their unconditional affection and acceptance. We feel a thrill when we glimpse wild creatures in their natural habitat or in our own backyard.

Unfortunately, the human-animal bond has at times been weakened. Humans have exploited some animal species to the point of extinction.

The Humane Society of the United States makes a difference in the lives of animals here at home and worldwide. The HSUS is dedicated to creating a world where our relationship with animals is guided by compassion. We seek a truly humane society in which animals are respected for their intrinsic value, and where the human-animal bond is strong.

Want to help animals? We have plenty of suggestions. Adopt a pet from a local shelter, or join The Humane Society and be a part of our work to help companion animals and wildlife. You will be funding our educational, legislative, investigative, and outreach projects in the United States and across the globe.

Or perhaps you'd like to make a memorial donation in honor of a pet, friend or relative? You can through our Kindred Spirits program. If you'd like to contribute in a more structured way, our Planned Giving Office has suggestions about estate planning, annuities, and even gifts of stock that avoid capital gains taxes.

Maybe you have land that you would like to preserve as a lasting habitat for wildlife. Our Wildlife Land Trust can help you. Perhaps the land you want to share is a backyard — that's enough. Our Urban Wildlife Sanctuary Program will show you how to create a habitat for your wild neighbors.

So you see, it's easy to help animals. And The HSUS is here to help.

The Humane Society of the United States
2100 L Street NW
Washington, DC 20037
202-452-1100
www.hsus.org

TABLE OF CONTENTS

CHAPTER 6: HOW WILL YOU TRADE?.................. 109

CHAPTER 7: THE FUNDAMENTALS.................... 117

CHAPTER 8: CAUGHT ON THE TECHNICALITIES... 133

FOREWORD

By Stuart McPhee

Trading would have to be one of the best professions available when you consider its benefits. It allows you to work for yourself with relatively little start up capital, there are very few overhead expenses, and now more than ever, you can execute trades almost seamlessly from anywhere in the world. These are the obvious attractions to trading with the single biggest attraction and primary motivation for most being the potential to make lots of money.

However, the biggest problem facing new traders is that many think trading is easy money. "How hard could buying and selling really be?" would be a common sentiment among newcomers. Unfortunately, trading is probably the hardest 'easy money' there is. Trading has relatively straightforward concepts that have stood the test of time, yet it is amazing how many people make a mess of it.

Like many endeavors in life, the actions required to trade well are often counter intuitive. If people are not aware of these issues, they often make all the same mistakes that so many people before them have made time and time again. Alan Northcott has taken great steps towards identifying the many challenges that new traders face; therefore, *The Complete Guide to Investing in Short Term Trading* is an excellent resource and should sit proudly with your collection of trading books.

Furthermore, Northcott has tackled a wide variety of topics, and consequently, has provided you a thorough overview of the many facets of setting up a trading methodology that is going to work for you. The rare approach of including several interviews within the book is a wonderful idea and provides you a valuable insight into the minds of those who have come before you and worked through the usual challenges.

Having read more trading books than I care to remember, and having presented to thousands of traders around the world, I feel that this book will assist anyone who needs to lay the foundations for long term, consistent, and profitable trading. It will also serve as a useful read for more experienced traders who feel the need to be reminded of the trading principles that work.

M2A-618953

4BQGBJ00D9L5

quickly and that you review your purchase below.

Title	THE COMPLETE GUIDE TO INVESTING
Condition	Very Good
Location	Aisle 65 Section 2 Shelf 11 Item 160
Description	A well-cared-for item that has seen limited use but remains in great condition. The item is complete, unmarked, and undamaged, but may show some limited signs of wear. Item works perfectly. Pages are intact and not marred by notes or highlighting. The spine is undamaged.
ASIN	160138002X
Employee	1782

If anything is incorrect, please contact us immediately at orders@jensononline.com and we will make it right. Thank you again for your purchase and please leave feedback online!

Stuart McPhee

Trading Coach

Melbourne, Australia

T: +61 3 8802 0593

W: **http://www.trading-plan.com**

Formally a full-time Australian Army officer, Stuart McPhee is now a private trader, author, and trading coach. His articles have been widely published and he is the proud author of *Trading in a Nutshell, 2nd Edition.* Living in Melbourne, Australia, Stuart regularly travels throughout Southeast Asia to conduct trading courses and has presented at numerous trading expos in Australia, Singapore, Malaysia, Vietnam, China, and Thailand. Stuart can be contacted through his 'Develop Your Trading Plan' Web site at **www.trading-plan.com.**

INTRODUCTION

The stock market — what images do these words conjure in the average American's mind? The majority of the public does not know what the stock market is all about. These people do not understand what makes it work. They look at the stock market numbers as if they are written in Latin. They wonder what makes them go up and down so drastically and so suddenly. Many people may think of investing, and indeed this is one way you can take advantage of the stock market. The most common form of investment in the United States is that associated with 401K retirement plans, but those may offer a limited selection of choices in funds, which reflect only a small section of the economic markets.

Now you have decided to leave these people behind and enter the ranks of the trader. Welcome and hold on tight, because you are in for the ride of your life. What is the purpose of trading? Why not just invest? Investing is a thing that everyone should do, and, as you read on, you will discover that investing and trading are different. Trading is about maximizing profit potential. If you do it right, you can make more money — plain and simple.

When envisioning the stock market, screens and newspaper pages full of lists of numbers, Wall Street, and businessmen in suits who sit at their desks in the corporate office buildings calling their broker, come to mind. This is all accurate. However, it is only part of the picture.

Trading on the stock market is not just reserved for industry players anymore. A new playing field has emerged, and it has changed forever the way the stock market is used. It has opened up the stock market to every person who wishes to go for the ride, and the Internet is the new playing field.

Yes, of course, the Internet. Not only has it revolutionized self-employment and the home-based business opportunity, the Internet has also revolutionized shopping, gaming, and the ability of people to educate themselves on just about any topic you can imagine. It has also brought the world of the trader into homes around the world. It does not matter if you are in an office on the 20th floor or in your own living room wearing pajamas. If you have a computer, you can trade. The Internet has made it possible to hold accounts online; transfer money with the click of a mouse button; and make decisions as to whether you should buy those pink shoes you were admiring, the golf clubs you saw on eBay, or the Chow Down Dog Food stocks that have just bottomed out. Your mouse may be the most powerful tool in your home and in your life, making it possible to change your life drastically. You must learn not to be click-happy in the trading game, ensuring that impulse is left at the door.

One fundamental tenet you must know right from the beginning is that investment and short-term trading are not the same thing. If you are planning to buy stocks based on a company's performance over the last decade and then park your money there, you have picked up the wrong book. This book is about short-term trading — what it is, how it works, and what does not work. It is about learning the necessary skills to play with the big boys who still reside on Wall Street and about which character traits will help you and which ones will hinder you.

Short-term trading can easily be summed up as trading in the stock market over a short period of time. There are three main types of short-term trading that you will learn about in the following pages. These are:

- Day trading (aka momentum or action trading and including scalping)

- Swing trading

- Position trading (aka core or trend trading)

Many short-term traders work during the day and do not hold positions overnight. However, there is another huge section that mainly trade "end of day," and these may hold positions for days or even weeks. This is a common way of entering the business while still holding down a full-time job. These different styles of trading will be discussed in this book. Suffice it to say here that, if you want the excitement, short-term trading can be an "on the edge of your seat, eyes on five indicators at once, finger poised over the mouse button, and eyes wide shut" experience, for which the best childhood preparation would have been honing your reactions with video games.

Every successful endeavor was once a goal. Goals are crucial to success, and this book is no different. The goal set when writing this book was to reach out to all those new and novice traders who might empty their bank accounts and even risk their homes and their way of life without the proper information on trading. The goal is also to bring you this information in a new and unique way. After all, there are many well-written books on short-term trading that you can, and maybe have, read. Most of them are written by experts, and they are full of the best information.

So what is different about this book? You will not just find one expert's voice in this book; you will find many experts' voices, all with valuable information to share with you. You will find that many chapters have Case Studies relating to the content in which you will be able to learn from the wisdom of one who has gone before you. These Case Studies are the real stories of some of the most successful traders in the business and ones who have been trading for years. They have seen success, and they have felt the sting of failure. They have had to develop their own systems, and they have had to learn strategies and techniques and discover their strengths and weaknesses to get to where they are today. They have contributed to this book so that you can learn from their mistakes and be inspired by their successes. You are sure to find that some of the stories resonate with you, and you will be able to identify with some of the people who are now successful. After all, people tend to be easily inspired by those who have gone before.

Knowing this, I wanted to bring to you a book that would in some way incorporate people who had come before. My words flow around their stories so that you can learn the ins and outs of the business through their experiences.

As you read, you will also learn valuable success strategies. These tips are well known, taught by the major success coaches of the world, and are crucial to the success of any endeavor. These strategies involve the use of the conscious and subconscious mind to remove barriers to success and to ensure that you will get everything you desire.

"Success Bullets" are included at the end of each chapter which summarize the key points that were covered in the chapter. These are the concepts you must be familiar with in your trading career before you step your cyber foot into the trading world, and they are what you must know on a daily basis to survive. These will be followed by terminology introduced in the chapter in the "Words to Know" section, and these terms are also included in the Glossary.

David Bach, in his book *Smart Women Finish Rich*, writes about a conversation he had with his mother when he was only five years old. He writes:

"I will never forget the moment I asked my mom, 'What makes the world go 'round — money or love?' I was only about five at the time. She looked me straight in the eyes and said, 'David, love is what makes life special, but without money you are in deep trouble.'"

Bach goes on to say that "trouble" was his substitute for the adult swearword his mother used, a word that truly made him understand the gravity of what she was saying to him. He never forgot what she told him, and I hope that you do not either. They are certainly words to live and plan your future by.

1

THE FIRE & THE BOTTOM LINE

EMOTION RULES

When most people think of cold, hard cash and the business world with its almighty bottom line, people think of men in business suits who have forgotten or choose not to care about the little guy and the hard-working family person. There is no warmth or love in the image of the business world where money is all that matters.

It is true that money is all that matters in the world of stocks and trades. However, you may be surprised to learn that, instead of being devoid of emotion, it is fueled by emotion. That is right. Those guys and gals on Wall Street, those suits in their corporate offices, and the day trader who sits in his or her home office every day control the market with their emotions.

You will find that the successful traders have had to learn how to rein in their emotions to trade. If you want to trade and you want to succeed, then you need to understand this above all else — your emotions can break you, especially greed and fear. They are the emotions that rule in trading. You need to leave these two emotions at the door to your office when you begin to trade each day, as they are powerful enough to allow you to ruin your financial life.

THE TWO MONSTERS

Greed

Greed may seem fairly straightforward. After all, money and greed have always gone hand in hand, right? Precisely. This could not be more true than in the stock market. But how specifically can greed do you in? How can it turn your world upside down? How can it control your every move (at least the ones that do not have fear tugging at them) and cause you major grief?

Picture this. You just bought 2,000 shares of King Tires, and you are watching eagerly on the five-minute chart as the stock climbs and climbs. You planned your entry point perfectly, and you were right on the money, so to speak. That stock responded just as you knew it would, based on the indicators. You go out for lunch, and you come back to find that the stock has broken through resistance and has reached an all-time high. However, you have just passed your exit point. You eye the screen and the indicators, and all looks good. "I will ride it out just a little longer," you think. After all, all signs are pointing to the rising of the stock, or are they? One or two indicators are suggesting there might be an issue. There seems to be a higher volume traded within the past five minutes, but you chalk that up to more people jumping on the bandwagon. Maybe they will drive thc pricc up further. Then, before your eyes, the stock plummets. You scramble, but your fingers can move only so fast, and by the time you are clicking to sell, there is no one left to sell to. Everyone who was in the lead has jumped ship, and those who are left, including you, are about to go to the watery depths below.

But you are sitting there saying, "I'm not greedy." It does not matter how down to earth you are, nor does it matter how well you manage your finances, how well you stick to your budget, or how easily you can overcome the temptation to spend half of your bank account on spring sales at the mall. The fact of the matter is that until you truly experience the market live and in the moment, you do not know what you are up against, and you may be in for a big surprise. If, on the other hand, you are greedy and you want to squeeze as much as you can out of the market, you need to rein yourself in. If you lack self-control, you will fail quickly.

Fear

Fear is the other and possibly the stronger influence of the two feelings. Fear comes in many forms. You might be afraid of losing your money. You might be afraid of what others, especially your family, think of your trading or what they will think if you lose money. You might be afraid of what other traders might think of your trades and your level of success. You might even be afraid of success. Whatever you fear, you need to know that allowing the feeling to control your moves can cause that feared scenario to manifest itself.

Not only do greed and fear drive your trading decisions if you are not careful, but they also have a major influence on the market as a whole. After all, you are not the only trader who has these two emotions. There are many traders out there who may not be as skilled as you will become at keeping these emotions in check. Bear in mind that up to 90 percent of would-be traders fail in the first six months of trying, so, although the best 10 percent will be in the business for longer, maybe years, there is still much inexperienced trading going on and pulling the short-term markets around. You can often see the greed pushing an uptrend higher and the fear driving the downtrend. Skilled traders know the signs, and they know when to jump in and when to pull back accordingly. It is a fact, and you will find the same theme echoed by all the successful traders in their Case Studies, that traders fail when they allow their emotions to override their planning.

THE OTHER EMOTIONS

All right, there are a few other emotions of which you need to be aware. The first of these is hope. Do not bring hope into the office. Leave it at the door because it has no place in the trader's day. The market does not ride on hope, and when you begin to hope, you begin to make unwise decisions. The same goes for optimism and faith. These emotions falsely allow you to think that there may be a trading god you can pray to for all your trading needs. There is not. These feelings can carry you, and they can lead back to the greed and fear mentioned earlier. Now, many of you may have heard that the opposite of fear is faith. This may be true in the rest of life but not in trading. In trading, they sit on the same side of the fence. The trading world is ruthless, and experienced traders know how to be ruthless. They will take your money if you do not trade wisely, and emotions can only precipitate that scenario.

GLOBAL INFLUENCE

The world has shrunk to the size of a computer screen. You can access anything, anytime, anywhere. It is unbelievable how quickly information travels in our technologically advanced society. Sometimes you learn about and even see the news as it is happening. The media is powerful, and this situation has a significant impact on the volatility of the markets.

First, a word about volatility. This is one of the few things you can count on in today's market. It is simply a word used to define rapid price change. Traders live for volatility because it is this factor that can usher in fat profits if the game is played properly. Volatility is what shoots stocks up and what causes them to plummet, so whether you are buying or selling short, you need to be aware of the global news and how it might affect you and your trades.

Every short-term trader will tell you that timing is of the essence in today's market. You must be quick, and you must be paying attention. You must be a Mexican jumping bean that has purpose and direction, jumping in and out of trades with a deftness that seems to defy reality. Oh yeah, and you have to have fast reflexes.

SUPPLY AND DEMAND

So what makes the market go up and down? Of course,

emotions like greed and fear help drive the market, and the global state of affairs and how it is reported in the media all push trends. But when it comes down to it, what powers the roller coaster?

If you have had even casual exposure to the field of economics, two words will be stuck in your mind - supply and demand. You may even have seen graphs picturing these variables against price – they are very simple in concept. The graph of supply v. price shows that supply increases as price goes up, because more people are prepared to put their resources into providing the product for greater returns. On the other hand, the demand graph shows that the demand for something decreases as the price goes up, as people will buy less. The theory goes that there is a balance point where, at one particular price, the supply and demand are equal, and the world is happy. Of course, in the real world there is seldom a perfect balance, so prices and quantities fluctuate around the perfect point.

However, this is what the stock market thrives on. Think of it as the stock market's breathing pattern, which can sometimes be erratic. When there is heavy action, the stock market can breathe rapidly, and trends can move up and down with lightning speed. On the other hand, when the stock market is at rest and relatively calm, you will see gentle uptrends followed by gentle downtrends. The uptrends begin when there is an abundant supply of stocks and the price is low. As demand rises and the supply gets eaten up, the price goes higher until the demand outstrips the supply for the stock and the turnaround happens. Then the price begins to drop as stocks are sold. Once the supply increases, this same cycle repeats itself.

SKILLS OF THE TRADE

Aside from not allowing fear and greed to influence your trading decisions, you must have or develop certain important skills to trade successfully. Many of these skills may be present in your personality and need only to be built up, and others are skills that you have always lacked for whatever reason. However, they are all skills that can be learned and honed to be of greatest benefit to your trading career. Traders are not born; they are made.

The first of these skills is the ability to stick with your plan. You already know that you should ride your gainers and get out of the losers, yet surprisingly it has been found that traders stay twice as long in their losers, going down, than they do in their winners when they are rising. Many studies have also found that quite a few traders do not make money and have to give up their trading, before, or tragically sometimes after, going broke. You do not want to join them, so you must learn the discipline of following your plan and conquering your human instincts, which want you to change the plan "on the fly" to fit in with your emotions at the time. It is a human instinct to want to be right, so if you thought you were right to buy in when you did, it is incredibly difficult to immediately sell if the price goes the wrong way.

A second skill that you will need to develop is adaptability. This may seem to run counter to the previous skill of being disciplined and sticking with your plan. Adaptability is important in developing and refining your trading system. No one has ever invented a perfect trading system, and if someone did it would not stay perfect for long. The best you can do is continual refinement, coupled with testing, to hone your own system. The stock market is one of the most unpredictable beasts there is. Although it often follows regular cycles, you need to work to keep the edge, which spells the difference between profit and loss. The reason for this is apparent if you think about it. If a system works well, others will start to use it, and you will lose the advantage. You need to be out there improving your system continuously on the basis of feedback from your successes and failures.

If your aim is to join the fast-moving society of the day trader, another crucial skill to develop is that of multi-tasking. Being able to do more than one or two things at a time is vital to your success. It is particularly important to be able to watch more than one or two things at a time. You will need your eyes on the candlestick charts, you will be watching the market moves, and you will be watching CNBC out of the corner of your eye as well.

BEING WRONG — GET USED TO IT!

Many of us need to be right. Face it. Do you ever push your point simply because you cannot admit when you have made a mistake and you are wrong? Yes, the need to be right and mistakes go hand in hand. In trading you had better learn humility and accept that you will make mistakes — lots of them. It is my hope that by reading this book and others like it, you will make mistakes that merely put a dent in your trading account rather than mistakes that will cost you your entire nest egg and your house, leaving you with nothing but the clothes on your back. Successful traders do not get it right all the time; it is not that simple a game. If it was, then everyone would be scoring big and there would not be the opportunity for you to make much money. What you must learn to do is limit your losses and ride your winners. Do not forget that short-term trading is a zero-sum game — what you buy or sell, someone else is selling or buying, and the short term seldom realizes any inherent value or growth in a stock. Take away the costs of trading from your profits, and it is no wonder that the majority of traders fail.

If you do not like making mistakes, maybe trading is not for you. It is not for everyone. If you are ready to accept that you will make mistakes, then you will need to admit it, which means that you will need to be wrong sometimes and learn your lessons. You will not always enter at the right point. It is hard to do all your analysis, wait for what your indicators and system tell you is the right moment, buy the stock and watch it reverse and go down. You must be able to say "Oh, well," sell when you hit your predetermined limit, and coolly examine if it was just one of those things or if you could refine your system to avoid the same set of circumstances in the future.

You will sometimes, especially in your early days of trading, ride a stock past your exit point because you have a "feeling" it is going to make you loads of cash. Then it will crash hard and, because you ignored the signs, you will pay — literally. Then you may have a difficult time looking back on the situation because when you do, you will see that the signs were all there and you did not heed them. Do you admit you were wrong and learn from your mistake, or do you pass this off to your colleagues as one that was "out of your control?"

You see, trading is a human game. After all, humans created money and the number system, and although numbers and money are considered to be logical, they are rarely so. Emotion controls money, and pride is an emotion. Needing to be right when your trading account or more is at stake, just to prove a point, well, it is your call. Even though you may not always enter at the lowest point or exit at the highest point (it is most unlikely that you will, and, you will be pleased to hear, you do not need to in order to make money), you should plan so that your money will be safe and you will be able to sleep at night.

USING YOUR BRAIN — BOTH SIDES

The stock market brings with it images of numbers, hundreds and thousands of numbers. Think of the logical business person, the strict discipline, and the ability to reason. Creativity and intuition are the furthest from your mind. However, it is creativity and intuition that may ultimately save your shirt and make you millions.

How is this so in such a numbers game? Although it is true that the stock market is all about numbers, it is the analysis of those numbers that determines how you respond to the market. By knowing what the numbers are saying, you will know whether to buy, sell, or sit on your hands and do nothing. The analysis of the numbers requires your creativity and intuition. Never forget that the other side of any trading is a human being, and, as stupid and illogical as people are, you cannot demand that stock prices act according to strict logic.

Let us put it in terms of your brain. Your brain is divided into the right hemisphere and the left hemisphere. The left hemisphere is the part of your brain that is responsible for logic and analysis. On the other hand, the right hemisphere is associated with the artistic and creative person. The following list is a breakdown of what each side of the brain is responsible for:

LEFT BRAIN

- Analysis

- Logic and ability to reason

- Writing

- Details

- Facts

- Words and language

- Present and past

- Math and science

- Comprehension

- Knowledge

- Acknowledgment

- Order/pattern perception

- Reality

- Object names

- Strategies

- Practicality

- Safety

RIGHT BRAIN

- Colors and shapes

- Symbols and images

- Imagination and fantasy

- Rhythm

- Daydreaming and emotions

- Intuition

- Usage of feeling

- "Big picture"

- Creativity

- Present and future

- Philosophy and religion

- Understanding of meaning

- Belief

- Appreciation

- Spatial perception

- Object functions

- Possibilities

- Impetuousness

- Risk

Take a look at the last word in each of these lists. Left brain = safety. Right brain = risk. In the trading world, you need to find and maintain a balance between playing it safe and taking risks. If you want to play it safe all the time, you may as well just put your money into long-term investments, and if you feel like taking risks all the time, you may as well hand over your money, house, car, and all your personal belongings on a silver platter.

Of course, there are plenty of facts that you must look at with every trading decision you make. With the left hemisphere of your brain you must look at the numbers. You must evaluate the volume of stocks moving at any given time, and you absolutely must determine at precisely which point you will enter and exit and where your stop-loss point will be. However, the main tool of any trader is the charts. Charts are covered in detail in Chapter 8 et al, but here we present what a chart is. It is a visual representation of those numbers. In the trading world, the chart is a visual representation of price and time and how the price changes over time. Once we get into the visual representation, the brain's right hemisphere can take over.

When you look at a chart, whether it is an intraday chart or a chart over a longer period, you are looking for an pattern to emerge that represents the behavior of the stock. The recognition of patterns, rhythms, and cyclical movement is all a function of the right hemisphere. The right hemisphere works with the big picture, and sometimes in the day trading world you have to step back so that you are able to see the big picture. By analyzing the patterns, you can let your intuition take over and get a feel for what will come next. Over time and with much experience, you will become efficient at making good trades.

WE ARE NOT TALKING SPORTS HERE

The bulls versus the bears. Although this sounds like a sporting event, it is far more competitive and cutthroat than that. The stock market is a fierce playing field, and those who are not bulls or bears and those who do not know how to play with the bulls and the bears will either get trampled or eaten alive. Thousands of dollars are won and lost every day, and most of the time the bulls and bears are winning. Can you stand the competition?

The system is quite simple. The bulls are the buyers. They create and take advantage of the uptrends in the market and believe prices will rise. The bears are the sellers. They work on the premise that the stock prices are going to fall, and they will make their profits from downtrends. When you follow the trends, you will become experienced as to whether you are looking at a bull market or a bear market. If the bulls are in charge, you buy. If the bears are in charge, you need to stand aside, unless you understand the finer points of selling short to make profits from declining prices.

The actions of these animals are controlled by greed and fear. Sometimes bulls and bears get into the ring together and there is a major battle for control. You do not want to be in the middle of that battle, especially if you are a new trader. You must know when to stand aside and watch. After all, there are two other animals in the stock market: the hogs and the sheep. The hogs get slaughtered because they are just plain greedy, and the sheep follow blindly, taking their lead from tips and tricks they pick up anywhere, and they end up losing big time.

SUCCESS BULLETS

- Emotions rule the stock market, especially those of the inexperienced trader.

- The most destructive emotions in the market game are greed and fear. These two monsters will rule your trades and break your account wide open unless you quickly learn to get a handle on them. If you think they will not be a problem for you, then you need to be extra cautious.

- The emotions of hope, faith, and optimism need to be left outside the office door as well.

- No matter how level-headed you are, greed and fear can still sneak up on you in the heat of the trading moment; never think you are immune, and do not go in with greed in mind.

- Global influence affects the volatility of the market. News is shared as it happens, and response can be almost instantaneous.

- Supply and demand determine the market direction. Demand drives the price up, and supply levels it out or causes it to drop.

- You can develop all the necessary skills to become a successful trader.

- You must learn to make a plan and stick with it.

- Adaptability is the name of the market game. With the volatility of the market, you must be able to change on a dime to make a dime or more. You must be able to know when to move and when to stay, and you must not be stubborn but change with the flow of the market river.

- When you accept that you can and will be wrong, you will take a big step toward becoming a successful trader.

- Despite the fact that the market is a numbers game full of analysis, this analysis uses the creative right side of our brains. It simply is not only about logic. Being able to see patterns and trends in the charts is crucial.

- Trading is a game of balance between taking risks and playing it safe. You must know which one to do when.

- The bulls and the bears control the market, and you must dance their dance or sit out if you do not want your toes stepped on.

WORDS TO KNOW

Bears, bulls, day trading, downtrend, exit point, indicators, short, trend, uptrend, volatility, volume

2

WHO CONTROLS IT ALL?

THE BROAD MARKETS

The stock market is a billion-dollar industry. Traders are active every working day of the week in these markets, and other markets, such as foreign exchanges, do not even sleep. The markets are the economical drive in the United States, and what they do the economy mimics. Wall Street dictates the mood of the day. If the markets soar, the economy soars with it. If the markets crash, the economy goes into a nose dive, and everyone needs to hold on, trader or not. Even if you are not a trader, the markets affect your life in a profound way.

Although the stock market is the main artery of the economy, it is by no means the only market available on which to trade. There are a few other markets that are important in the grand scheme of things. Although most of our discussion in this book will center on the stock market, the same principles will apply to other trading markets. It is important to have some background knowledge on the various broad markets available today.

STOCK MARKETS

Stocks are simply shares in a company. When you own stocks you are a part owner of the company whose stocks you have purchased. However, like you, most people do not own enough shares in a company to be involved in the decision-making. Most people buy shares simply with the hopes that they will increase in value and return a nice profit. The money that changes hands during these trades does not go directly to the companies but to the people selling the shares.

The shares of almost every publicly traded company in the United States and many companies outside of the United States are traded on one of the stock exchanges. There are some regulatory issues with trading stocks in the markets of different countries, but it is much more possible than it used to be because of Internet access. For instance, it is possible to trade stocks on the LSE (London Stock Exchange) using an online broker such as Selftrade — you need only a Great Britain bank account and a physical address, which can be anywhere in the world.

Trading stocks is an excellent place to start your trading education, even if you decide to go into other financial instruments later — there are many stocks from which to choose, and buying and selling is straightforward and commonplace.

BOND MARKETS

Bonds are loans. When you buy a bond you are lending the company (or the government) money. This means that for each bond you buy you are holding a piece of the company's debt. You are then paid a certain amount of interest for the period of time you hold the bond. Thus, with bonds, there is no ownership of a company. However, they are considered a safer investment than stocks because when a company files for bankruptcy, bond holders are higher up in the pecking order. In other words, they get paid out before the stock holders. As bonds are only debts, and not ownership in the company, they are not suitable for trading in the way that stocks are.

FUTURES MARKET

The futures market got its start in Japan in the 18th century. This market is not based on shares in a company but on a commodity or product itself and a prediction of what its value will be at a given time in the future. The original products were agricultural but have expanded to include oil and minerals.

Futures are sold on contract between a seller, which is the producer or manufacturer, and the buyer, which is the consumer. When you buy a futures contract you are agreeing to buy a product for a set price at a certain date in the future. This product is not yet for sale and may not yet have been produced. On the other hand, when you sell a futures contract, you are agreeing to provide that product at the specified price at a certain date in the future. Clearly, there is risk associated with futures, as you are committed to the contract regardless of what the price does — you want to have your crystal ball well polished. That said, if you become proficient at futures trading, the opportunities for profit are substantial.

It is common for people to buy a futures contract even though they have no intention of using the product. They will then sell the contract to a third party before the delivery date indicated on the contract.

OPTIONS MARKET

The options market is another market bound by contracts. The options contract gives the buyer the right, but not the obligation, to either buy or sell the asset named in the contract at the specified price on or before the date specified in the contract. In common with futures, the option contract has an expiration date, and if the buyer decides not to buy or sell the asset by that date, then that person will lose his entire initial investment in the option — there is no value at all after the date passes. However, this is all that is at risk, so it is somewhat safer than futures trading. Unlike futures, there is no compulsion to make the sale or purchase. If the buyer guesses correctly, the option leverages his or her initial investment, as he or she has control of the certain number of shares for much less than buying the shares, so this can be a path to greater profits. Options are in the family of "derivatives," as are futures. Derivatives are any financial instrument that "derives" its value from another but does not include direct ownership of the other. Thus futures may derive their value from commodities, but you do not own any commodity in buying the futures contract.

Brian McAboy is familiar with options and trades seasonally, as you can see from his Case Study.

SUCCESS STORY: BRIAN MCABOY

Brian McAboy is a retired Quality Engineer, trader, and author of *The Subtle Trap of Trading.* Brian helps traders develop the right mind-set, skills and practices to get the most out of their trading, both personally and financially. For free videos on how to become a successful in trading and to get your free copy of "The Seven Traits of Winning Traders," visit **http://InsideOutTrading.com**.

What types of trading are you involved with?	My preference is largely seasonal trend-following in the futures markets, trading with options. Trades are usually anywhere from one week to four months, depending on the market.
How did you start trading?	Got a call from a broker back in 2000 and bought three out of the money call options on unleaded gas. Apparently he got my name from me being on Ken Roberts' mailing list from years before. I studied the yearly charts on unleaded and saw a very repeatable price cycle from winter to June-July, so I decided to give it a go. I had not really thought about trading up to that point, but the lure got me, just like most people. I missed my target sell price by two days and wound up losing $3,300.
What were your main concerns when starting trading?	Not having a clue as to what I was doing, thus relying heavily on my broker's recommendation.
How soon did you see a steady flow of income?	Not until 2004 when I began trading on a regular basis. Prior to that I just dabbled here and there as money was available.
What are your likes and dislikes about trading?	Likes: Personally I think trading is by far the best business in the world for a person to pursue. It has all the upsides one could ask for and very few downsides. Additionally, trading provides a tremendous education that is not likely to be found in any other pursuit — you will learn a ton about macroeconomics, plus you will learn things about yourself that are extremely valuable — if you will pay attention. I think everyone should try trading simply because of all that you will learn. Very, very valuable experience, plus if you make it as a trader, you will be good at the best business on the planet for individuals. It offers freedom, independence, open to anyone, anywhere, at any age. You can trade part time, full time or even trade as you travel the world, plus it is recession-proof, and it will never be obsolete.

SUCCESS STORY: BRIAN MCABOY	
	Dislikes: The way that most people are introduced to trading. Most are told that trading is easy money and "get rich quick," neither of which are true. If people entering trading were given the right information when they start, the failure rate in trading would only be 20-30 percent instead of the ~90 percent that it is currently and has been for decades. There are several aspects of trading as a business pursuit that really favor the person that is aware of them and will simply take advantage of these aspects. Instead, most are simply prompted to get busy trading and lose their money before they figure out what they need to know.
What personal qualities helped you to become a trader?	Persistence and my understanding of business development and how people work. Also, it is the approach to the whole matter that makes the difference. Trading is a mental game, so understanding that it all begins and ends with you and your mind-set is where success is found.
What is the biggest challenge you have faced in trading?	The intellectual appeal of trading. Most traders are smarter than average, and the intellectual challenge to beat the markets makes it always tempting to overcomplicate the matter. Keeping things simple is one of the keys to making it work.
What advice would you give potential traders?	Again, trading is a mental game. Focus on yourself in three primary areas: emotional control, building skills, then establishing and following good practices. That is why I focus on these three areas at my site, **InsideOutTrading.com**
What qualities do you think are important in a would-be trader?	I actually wrote a report about this titled, "The Seven Traits of Winning Traders." You can get a free copy at **http:// InsideOutTrading.com**
When did you know that you would be successful?	In 2004 when I realized what I note above — when I began focusing on the three primary areas and being patient enough to work through them.
Describe your typical day.	It varies considerably. Most days I am not trading, as I trade part time in markets that I know, and I know when to trade them due to their seasonality.
What is the biggest trading mistake you ever made?	Hanging on to my crude oil contracts in early 2004. I simply knew that the market would continue to run, despite all the indicators that it was time to take profits. I lost over $32,000 with that one.

SUCCESS STORY: BRIAN MCABOY	
Which stock indicator do you pay the most attention to?	I do not trade stocks anymore.
Describe your setup of computer, software, and Internet connection.	I work on a Dell machine (been a fan of Dell's for over 10 years now) with broadband Internet access. I use a custom trading software and the Trading Performance Analyzer to run my system metrics and for tracking my trading performance. Trading system metrics are one of the keys for all successful traders, both as an emotional safeguard and for continuous improvement and consistency.

FOREX MARKETS

Forex is short for foreign exchange, in other words, dealing with currencies of different countries and exchange rates. This is an intriguing market, as it never sleeps and has no central exchange. In some ways, it is easier than trading, as you have to deal only with the difference between buy and sell prices and not commissions. It is also huge, for all practical purposes unlimited in scope, unlike individual stocks, which, particularly in the penny stock area, can be somewhat illiquid and subject to volume effects.

COMMODITY MARKETS

The commodity markets are easier to understand, as they involve the buying and selling of raw materials, such as farm crops, livestock, and energy. In other respects, they are like trading on the stock market. Obviously, commodities can be affected by other than trading forces, as for instance the weather may reduce or increase crops and provide an influence external to the market on supply and demand.

THE TREE OF GREED AND FEAR

Can you believe that the first trades on Wall Street were performed under a tree? In the beginning, all buying and selling was completed under a sycamore tree at 68-70 Wall Street. But I am getting ahead of myself here. Wall Street was named as such because it originally ran alongside a wall. This wall was first built to control the cows running around in Manhattan, and later it was fortified as a defense against the British. Wall Street is still about control, but now it is about financial control.

Back to the sycamore tree. The government issued notes, and other stocks, bonds, and orders for commodities, which were sold to the public. Many shares were sold to people who essentially helped build the foundation of American companies. In 1792, the stock market began trading formally. The original club of 12 brokers still met under a tree (a buttonwood tree) or inside the local Tontine Coffee House. They were extremely competitive and strove to protect their own interests rather than the interests of their customers. With the public outcry, brokerages were formed to protect public interests by offering shares at fair prices.

By 1827, the stock market, in the form of the New York Stock Exchange, found a home inside a building, and this was followed by the opening of the American Stock Exchange in 1842. Thus, the face of trading was changed forever, and Wall Street became a financial force to be reckoned with.

EVOLUTION HAPPENS TO ALL CREATURES

The stock market is a creature that breathes, sleeps, and sometimes devours its participants. As such, it has evolved extensively since its conception in the 1700s. After all, you do not see a bunch of mad brokers under a tree anymore. No, now there are many players in the stock market that make for a wide and varied playing field. The three largest players in the market are the New York Stock Exchange (NYSE), the NASDAQ, and the American Stock Exchange (Amex).

THE STOCK EXCHANGES

The New York Stock Exchange (NYSE)

The NYSE has always been run under the principle that the customers are most important and that their orders are to be handled fairly and efficiently. In other words, the interests of the investor are to come first. It is run as a floor-based, central auction system, and it also operates as an electronic market. In 2006 the NYSE merged with ArcaEx and the Pacific Stock Exchange and now trades as a hybrid market.

Imagine the floor of the NYSE. Different "posts" or stations litter the floor of the NYSE, and one stock can be represented only at one particular station. At each of these stations is what you call a specialist, someone who acts almost like an auctioneer and literally conducts a two-way auction between buyers and sellers. This specialist also creates a market for the stock. Each stock only has one specialist, but each specialist can represent more than one stock. To keep life interesting, although it may seem as though the specialists rule the roost, all buy and sell orders are delivered to the floor electronically, and their Direct+ (a system in the NYSE that allows low volume trades without the intervention of the specialists) and automatic systems are the standard for filling a large percentage of their orders.

The NASDAQ

The NASDAQ, which once stood for the National Association of Securities Dealers Automated Quotations but now is used as a word in its own right and not an abbreviation, opened in February 1971, and it is the leading completely electronic stock market in the United States. The NASDAQ is a publicly traded company itself. The NASDAQ has no floor, but it has a big billboard. The electronic billboard is on the corner of 43rd and Broadway in New York City's Time Square. It constantly displays the frenzy of market news and advertisements. To the average person in New York, this represents the stock market because it is such a common scene. The NASDAQ trades in many different industries, but it has a reputation for being the ultimate technology market. It is also well known for its volatility, and as such, it is the day trader's playground. However, when you are new to the game, you may be better off starting out with the calmer NYSE.

Instead of specialists, the NASDAQ has what are known as "market makers." The NASDAQ itself is a single electronic system, and the market makers often represent the brokerage houses that trade in the market, although they can also operate independently. The market makers buy and trade on behalf of the clients of the brokerage houses, and they maintain liquidity in a stock as well. This is different from the NYSE, in which only one specialist works with a specific stock and is the only one making trades with that stock. With the NASDAQ, each stock can be traded by multiple market makers, which is one of the causes of the volatility of stocks. When decimalization came into play, the spread between the bid and ask prices grew smaller, which reduced the market makers' profits. The playing field became more level with the introduction of the direct-access platform, which allowed individual traders to take part in the fun. There are four types of market makers. They include:

- **Wholesale market makers** — These are the market makers that serve the institutions and those brokers and dealers who are not registered as market makers in a particular company's stocks but are required to fill orders for their clients with those particular stocks.

- **Retail market makers** — These market makers serve the institutions and individual investors who need orders filled. They ensure that there is a constant flow of orders.

- **Institutional market makers** — These market makers exist for the sole purpose of taking care of the needs of the institutional investor. They deal in large blocks of orders, and their clients include mutual funds or pension funds companies, insurance companies, and asset management companies.

- **Regional market makers** — These market makers live up to their name. They serve the needs of institutions and individuals in a specific geographical location. By focusing on the region, the market makers are able to offer better exposure to stocks in that particular area of the country.

Listing on the NASDAQ requires that companies meet minimum requirements. These requirements include minimum amounts in stockholder equity and income, a minimum bid price, a minimum number of shareholders, and a minimum number of publicly held shares with a minimum value. For those companies that do not meet the minimum requirements to be listed on the NASDAQ, they can be traded as over-the-counter or bulletin board (OTCBB) stocks. These stocks are more difficult to buy and sell, as market makers do not trade them, although you can find real-time quotes, last-sale prices, and volume information for these stocks.

The American Stock Exchange (Amex)

The Amex is the third most active exchange in the United States. It is made up of the stocks that are too small to be traded on the larger NYSE. Many of the companies that list on the Amex do so until they meet the requirements of the larger NYSE, and then they move to that exchange. Although the Amex trades in a fashion similar to the NYSE (it makes use of specialists too), it trades in equities, options, and exchange-traded funds (ETFs). The Amex Composite Index will give you a good indication of how the Amex is doing as a whole.

Other Exchanges

Besides these big contenders in the world of the exchanges, there are also regional centers that are committed to listing stocks for a particular geographical location. These are known as regional exchanges, and they exist in places such as Boston, Chicago, the Pacific, and Philadelphia. They can list stocks that are not listed elsewhere and those that are also listed on the larger exchanges.

WHO SHINES THE SPOTLIGHT?

CNBC, that is who. The CNBC television network is the source of all market news and happenings. If you want the inside scoop, this is where to get it. It operates in real time, just like the stock market itself. Of course, there are other reliable and even crucial ways to remain in the market news loop. CNN is a source for financial news, as are the Bloomberg television and radio networks. There are also a slew of financial papers that are a must read for the financial professional.

You must always take care when listening to the financial news on CNBC or anywhere else. The bottom line is if stocks run due to the news, then it will be because the amateur traders are pushing them up, up, up. They are acting on the quick words of some guru and their own lack of experience. Although you may occasionally see an important announcement regarding the financial state of affairs in the United States, you will more likely see the various commentators interviewing the financial experts on a regular basis. These are the mutual fund managers, the technical advisors, the CEOs of companies, and the authors of the many how-to financial books.

Experienced traders know to sit on their hands when they hear some brilliant market forecast. After all, if the CEO of some new company comes on and endorses it as the next Microsoft, there will be plenty of buying action. Unfortunately, this is often followed by a sudden and steep plummet.

When there is significant market news, it is typical to have this news leak out early in the morning and be bandied about by the experts. Buying has been going on during this time. Then CNBC announces the news. You must realize that CNBC is not the first source for the news. There are professional news systems that have delivered this news to the inside players in the system, long before CNBC has its say. This means that the professionals on the inside have been able to act on this news long before you even hear about it. They have already bought, so when the news does come out on CNBC and other financial networks, those inside professionals get to ride the wave and clean up on the rush of buying that takes place. This rush of buying drives the prices up, and then the insiders sell out and the crash happens, leaving those who jumped on the bandwagon just slightly stunned if they are lucky and crushed under the weight of the cart if they are not.

This is not to say that you should just ignore the news and that it will do nothing except clean out your trading account. However, it is important to take everything you hear on the financial news stations with that proverbial grain of salt. You will know soon enough if you made the right decision, and in the stock market it is sometimes live and learn.

EXCHANGE-TRADED FUNDS

Exchange-traded funds, or ETFs, have a major place in the trading world of today and deserve special mention here. They are rapidly becoming the new way to trade. ETFs are basically a single "stock" that in reality represents a group of stocks. In other words, each ETF represents a specific industry group, such as banks or technology, or ETFs can represent the stock indexes, such as the NASDAQ or the Dow. They can also represent a country as a whole.

By trading in ETFs, you can specify a target group in which you want to place your money. As this is currently a relatively new way to trade, they do not yet have a significant enough trading volume to allow for precise entries and exits. Because they combine many values, ETFs tend to be more stable than individual stocks, and they are worth looking into if you want to be involved with the stock market while minimizing the risk.

SUCCESS BULLETS

- The broad markets include the stock markets, the bond markets, the futures markets, the options markets, and Forex and commodity markets.

- The three largest players in the market are the New York Stock Exchange (NYSE), the NASDAQ, and the American Stock Exchange (Amex).

- The NYSE and the Amex are run by specialists, the NASDAQ by market makers.

- The NYSE and the NASDAQ list in stocks and the Amex lists in equities, options, and Exchange-traded funds (ETFs).

- CNBC and other financial sources of news can affect the market drastically. Take all news in calmly, and do not jump on the bandwagon unless you are sure (although being sure in the stock market is rare).

- Exchange-traded funds are the newest and fastest growing way to trade. They allow a trader to trade multiple stocks in one "stock."

WORDS TO KNOW

Amex, ask, bid, bonds, broker, direct-access platform, equities, ETF, Forex, futures, market makers, NASDAQ, NYSE, options, OTCBB, specialists, stocks

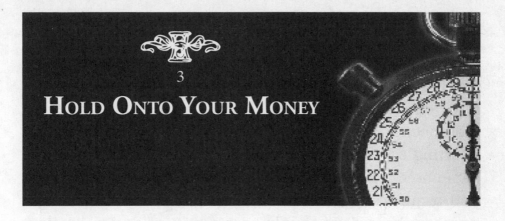

3

HOLD ONTO YOUR MONEY

Do not make a single trade until you are sure you understand how to read the market. There are many aspects of analyzing the market that you need to be aware of before you make that first trade, otherwise your first trade may be your last. This is your first lesson. In this chapter, you will learn all about the different types of trading that you can try. At this stage in your knowledge, I would invite you to start thinking about what sort of trading would suit your character, life style, and desires; after all, when you are successful you will be doing it instead of normal employment, and you want something that you can live with.

MEET THE TRADERS

What distinguishes the various types of traders is the amount of time they hold their position and the amount of risk involved in the trades they make. You can hold your position for seconds to minutes, weeks to months, or for any length of time in between. Of course, if you are trading every few seconds or minutes, you will find it a lot more intense than if you hold your position for a few days or weeks, but the potential could be great.

THE DAY TRADER

Day trading includes scalping, momentum, and action trading, and these all have the timespan in common but have different approaches to making a profit. Take, for instance, a scalper trying to sell last-minute tickets to a sporting event or a concert. The trading scalper is of the same breed. To be a scalper you must have quick reflexes and a quick reaction time. These day traders are few in number these days simply as a result of decimalization. Once upon a time, back in the illustrious '90s, the spread in the daily price ranges was wide, and scalpers executed hundreds and even thousands of trades per day. Talk about being busy.

The idea behind scalping is to buy or short a stock with the goal of taking a small profit from each transaction. Scalpers work in the time of seconds to minutes. The time is tight and the ride is fast so if you want to be a scalper, you had better be able to hold on with one hand because the other one will be clicking the mouse button furiously. Scalpers take profits from as low as one eighth to one quarter of a point, which means that scalpers also tend to buy in larger lots of shares. They will not trade in blocks of fewer than 1,000 shares simply because the profits would be so small they would not be worth it after taking out the fees and commissions.

Although the scalper is a type of day trader, there are other types of day traders who open and close trades within the span of a single trading day, and they trade on trends varying throughout the day. They are also known as momentum traders. Intraday trends are crucial to success, and trades are in equities, stocks, index futures, or ETFs. Positions are held from minutes to hours, and focus is needed for successful trades. When you are a momentum trader, you will be required to hold a $30,000 minimum amount in cash in your trading account at all times. This amount is steep, but it is a necessary cushion. Lot size for shares is commonly 500 to 1,000 shares or more per trade, and the average range of the stock is at least one point over the day. This is a time-intensive way to trade.

There are two types of active day traders: the institutional day trader and the retail day trader. They both tend to make a career out of trading, and they help maintain liquidity in the market with the trading techniques they use.

THE INSTITUTIONAL DAY TRADERS

The institutional traders are the specialists of NYSE and Amex and the market makers of the NASDAQ. The specialists are all members of the exchange they work with, and they act either as an individual, in a partnership, or as a part of a corporation. These specialists are responsible for the markets themselves, and they perform three key functions. They make the markets in certain exchange-traded securities, maintain the inventories of the securities, and ensure the market for their securities runs smoothly and is in good order.

The market makers of the NASDAQ are responsible for maintaining the liquidity and the efficiency of the stocks as well as the OTC stocks. They may be members of a brokerage firm or a bank that deals in the buying and selling of stocks, and they must be ready to buy and sell stock on a regular and consistent basis.

Specialists and market makers both execute trades in mere seconds and trade throughout the entire day.

THE RETAIL DAY TRADERS

Retail day traders take a completely different approach to making money. These are the individual investors who trade in the markets all day, executing many trades in a day. These are the traders who do not hold any position overnight but instead close out and sell all of their stocks at the end of the day. These are the people who could be trading while wearing their pajamas at 2 p.m. These traders prefer to use the electronic communication network (ECN), as it allows making trades at good prices easier and faster.

THE SWING TRADER

Swing traders are not bound by the clock or the end of the trading day. Thus, they will hold positions overnight and over weekends. This type of trading falls in between day trading and position trading (described next). Swing trading is a little less intense, as positions are held for two to five days and may be held for some weeks. It has become one of the most popular trading styles, as traders endeavor to ride the strong trend for as long as it lasts. This may be the most diverse crowd of traders. It includes those with full-time jobs who research when they are not working their day job. You can become a swing trader with a smaller account size.

As trends are the important factor for swing traders, the bulk of their trading time is spent researching rather than sitting in their chair ready to click, unlike the day trader. They must be technically savvy and have a deep understanding of the markets within which they trade. Swing traders rely more on brokers than they do on direct-access systems, and they are always looking for the strong uptrend or strong downtrend. They are not dependent on the intraday charts and may even rely on end-of-day charting software and information provided by their broker. The ultimate goal is for their positions to move from one to multiple points.

Swing traders trade in blocks of 1,000 shares, although they are not bound by this rule. They also do not hold more than ten positions at the same time. Unlike the position trader, the swing trader is looking for stock that will move right away or in the near future. They use a variety of criteria to analyze the stock trends and on which they base their trading decisions. These include:

- **Volume and liquidity** — Swing traders want to trade in actively traded and large stocks. They also want stocks that are easy to work with, as they need to be able to make their trades quickly.

- **Trending** — Swing traders are also looking for trending stocks. This means stocks that are obviously moving in an upward or downward pattern rather than straight across in a plateau (The significance of this topic will be addressed in Chapter 9).

- **Volatility** — Swing traders look for volatility in stocks as well. They want to see stocks that are moving a lot over the short term so they can profit quickly.

- **Sector selection** — Swing traders look to trade stocks in the strongest sectors, but they do use the weaker sectors for shorting stocks, or profiting from the weakening price.

- **Tight spreads** — Swing traders are also fully aware of the spread, or the difference between the bid and the ask when trading. The wider the spread, the lower the profits that can be made. The lower the stock price, the smaller the spread needs to be to maintain relative profits. Traders look for a small spread for greater profitability.

THE POSITION TRADER

Position trading is short-term investing. I am talking about holding positions for weeks to months. These traders jump on at the base of a trend and ride it all the way, or they jump off when it starts to go down, selling while the profit is still good. This type of trading requires the least amount of attention and effort. A position can be maintained and an automatic stop (to close your order if the price drops too low) can be decided upon and entered automatically or in consultation with your broker. All you need to do is check daily to ensure you are still in the proper trend. A small account size is acceptable for the position trader, and you are looking for your positions to move multiple points.

The position trader is interested in a combination of fundamental and technical analysis, as he or she wants a stock that is headed in the right direction and wants to choose the right time to buy.

MARKET PRICING

When you wish to execute a trade you will see something like this: Bid: 22.34, Ask: 22.35. Although this may look foreign, it is fairly straightforward. The bid at $22.34 is the inside bid, which is the highest price you can demand if you want to sell your shares.

On the other hand, the ask at $22.35 is the inside ask, or the lowest price at which you can buy shares. The spread is known as the difference between the bid and the ask. All of these numbers are referred to as "Level I" quotes.

When you use an online broker, you will be dealing in Level I quotes, and these are the usual type that you will encounter in normal investing. However, when you decide to be a trader, buying and selling in a short space of time, you can use a direct-access trading platform where you will have access to the Level II order-entry system. This system allows you to see all of the market participants for any stock you are trading. The market participants are others who want to sell or buy stocks at any particular time, and the Level II screen lists them together with the prices at which they are prepared to sell or buy, which will range above the inside ask and below the inside bid. Thus these participants are waiting for a price change in their favor before making the transaction.

This is where the serious day traders need to be. The scalpers and momentum traders will benefit the most from the Level II system. This is advantageous because with Level II access you can see the bid and ask from all of the participants, not only the inside bid and the inside ask.

ANALYZE THIS

Analysis is the name of the game. If you do not like analysis or you cannot get your mind around it, then close this book and find another way to earn money. You cannot trade without analysis. There are two types of analysis: fundamental and technical. Fundamental analysis is extremely useful for determining what sector to trade in, and technical analysis then takes over to follow the trends in that sector.

Here is a description of what each type of analysis can do for you.

FUNDAMENTAL ANALYSIS

This type of analysis will help you:

- Determine which part of the business cycle is driving the market at any given moment or time period.

- Determine which sector is the best choice for you in terms of trading.

- Determine which sectors are poised to move up.

- Determine which stocks are the top ones to watch on the ascending sectors.

- Understand what the Federal Reserve board feels about the economy and understand what things it does that can affect the markets.

- To do some "crystal ball gazing" and determine to some extent what potential shocks to the markets exist by looking for the right signs.

TECHNICAL ANALYSIS

Get into the nitty-gritty. With technical analysis, you can:

- Understand the technical conditions of the market and learn to trade within them.

- Use index charts to determine what the economic cycle is in the market.

- Determine when an ascending sector is stuck or ready to move into another uptrend.

- Determine when leading stocks are stuck or whether they are ready to move into another uptrend.

- Anticipate potential trend reversals.

Some traders will swear that you need to be concerned

only with technical analysis to trade effectively, and this is true for the short-term horizon, which dominates trading. However, when you are dealing over a longer term such as with position trading, then fundamental analysis becomes increasingly important as a tool to use to make good trading decisions. Thus Chapter 7 will present fundamental analysis in detail. The majority of the rest of this book will be dedicated to technical analysis because of its importance to the short-term trader.

SUCCESS BULLETS

- It is important to study the market before doing any trading.

- Day traders look for price changes each day and do not hold shares overnight.

- Scalpers look for small profits with rapid trading.

- Momentum traders are day traders who capitalize on intraday trends.

- Institutional day traders are members of the exchanges, or employed by banks and brokerages, and are responsible for the markets.

- In contrast, the retail day trader is an individual trader who may work from home.

- Swing traders look at a longer time span than day traders and may hold shares for days or weeks. They look for stocks with strong trends or other reasons for buying.

- Swing traders are also concerned with the trading volume and liquidity of the stocks they buy, as well as wanting volatility for quick profits.

- The position trader is a short-term investor and concerned with fundamental analysis as much as technical analysis. The fundamentals show him or her which stocks to consider; the technical analysis helps him or her decide on the right time to buy.

WORDS TO KNOW

Intraday, momentum trading, position trading, scalping, swing trading, technical analysis

4

PLACE YOUR ORDERS PLEASE

There are many different orders that you can give during your trading day. The idea of placing orders, rather than just calling your broker every time you want to buy and sell, is that these orders offer you protection. For example, a call to your broker to sell stock takes time, and if the stock is falling fast, you want out fast. The time it takes to get your broker on the phone may have been more than you wanted to take to place the sell order. When you first buy the stocks, if you set up a price at which you want to sell automatically if the stock goes down, then you can sit back and relax a little. You will know that your stock will be sold promptly and your money is safe.

If you do not use stop orders, you are vulnerable to overlooking a problem while otherwise occupied and losing more than you had planned. However, many people counsel against setting up automatic stops and prefer you exit manually when your stop price is reached, so that you stay in touch with your stocks and do not "tip your hand" on your exit strategy. A preset stop may also sell you out of a stock on the basis of a midday low, when the closing prices would not have, and this might upset your plan. Whether you set stops may depend on the length of your trades — the type of trader you are — but when you are starting you may have enough to distract you. Set up stop orders as soon as you buy a stock.

You must be familiar with the terminology of the different orders so that you can effectively manage your trading portfolio. The following is a comprehensive list of the types of orders that you can place throughout a trading day.

MARKET ORDER

A market order is the most basic type of order. This is the call to your broker to tell him to buy or sell stock at the current market price. Unless you give different instructions, this is the way your broker will carry out any order. The nice thing about the market order is that it is almost guaranteed to take place, or be filled, as long as there are buyers and sellers available. The order will be filled at the ask if it is an order to buy and at the bid if it is an order to sell. Your broker is key to getting the best price. Some brokers have special smart-order routing systems, which enable them to find the best ask and bid prices available. If you are trading on the NYSE, you may need a SuperDOT broker for this.

The good thing about market orders is that they are the least expensive to place. Unfortunately, the downside to market orders is that they are often filled at a price different from the one that was in effect at the time you placed the order. Everyone is working as fast as humanly possible, but most of the time humans do not move as fast as the market does. So when you put an order in with your broker, by the time he fills the order, the price will likely have shifted.

This means that you could be paying more than you had planned when buying or getting less than you had hoped when selling. This is called slippage. For instance, you call your broker and order 500 shares of A1 Software, which has an ask price of $14.60. By the time the order is put in and your broker calls you back to confirm, you have paid $14.70 per share. That is $0.10 more per share than you were planning on spending, and that equals $50 for the 500 shares you purchased. If you have two or three of those in a day you will feel it. There are some brokers and market makers who may take advantage of this slippage to line their own pockets, so beware. You can protect yourself from this by using a Level II screen through a direct-access broker or by issuing a limit order.

LIMIT ORDER

A limit order is all about limits, as you determine and enter the limits at which you will buy and sell. A limit order will allow you to avoid the problems associated with market orders that cause you to buy at higher prices than you wanted or sell at lower prices than you had intended. When you place a limit order, you specify the price at which you wish to buy and/or sell a particular stock. This is good protection. It means that the order will be filled only if the buying price is equal to or lower than your maximum limit and the selling price is equal to or higher than your minimum limit.

There is a downside to the limit order. There is a chance that the order will never be filled. If your buying limit price is never reached, you might never buy any of the stock that your analysis shows will make you money.

For instance, there is stock that you want to buy and you call your broker or place a limit order online. Your limit is to buy at the price of $14.50, but by the time you put in the order, the price has risen beyond that, and it never goes that low again. At least when you are buying the stock directly, you miss out on a potentially profitable trade only when you are selling. A limit order can be more problematic. If your selling limit price is never reached, you might be stuck with stock you do not want anymore. You want to be out of the trade, as the price keeps dropping, but your limit order says that you want a certain minimum price.

Another downside to the limit order is that brokers charge a higher fee to execute these orders. Be sure you know what the fee and commission structures are before you leap in.

STOP ORDER

This is an important type of order for your peace of mind and the security of your portfolio. This type of order is placed to avoid taking too much of a loss or to protect your profits. Once the price specified in the stop order is reached, the stop order automatically becomes a market order and is filled as soon as possible. What this means is that you do not have to watch the market every second of every day. You can relax a little, knowing that your investment is reasonably safe.

The downside to the stop order: although your peace of mind may be intact for the most part, here is the problem. If the market has a bad day due to bad news, and it does from time to time, it may plummet temporarily, causing your stop order to be activated. Then the stock recovers and the temporary downtrend reverses and soars. Meanwhile, you have to scramble to repurchase the stock and may end up having to buy it at a higher price than you had originally paid.

Another minus for the stop order is that once your stop order price is reached, it becomes a market order, and a market order can give you trouble too. If the stock is bottoming out quickly you may end up selling the shares at a price far lower than that of your original stop order because your broker simply could not move fast enough.

On the other hand, a stop order can be a good way to get into a trade. If you issue a stop order to buy at a level above the current price, this will not be triggered until the stock price rises, which, if you read the charts right, will be the start of a run upward. If the run does not happen, you do not buy the stock needlessly.

Stop orders are orders you can place on the exchanges; you cannot place one on the NASDAQ. In this case, your broker must watch the market and must place the order when he or she sees the limit price has been reached. Some brokers will not accept stop orders on certain securities, and it is rare for them to accept a stop order for OTC-traded stocks. For this reason, you should always check with your broker to make sure he or she accepts stop orders, and make sure to know the fees. You also want to understand how your broker's stop orders work so that you are sure to get precisely what you want out of them.

STOP-LIMIT ORDER

To reduce the risk of a stop order, place a stop-limit order. This type of order combines the stop order and the limit order. With the stop-limit order, when your stop price is reached, your order will not become a market order. Instead, it will become a limit order. This offers the most security, but there is a chance that your order remains unfilled if the prices fluctuate wildly. Again, these orders are more commonly used on the exchanges.

TRAILING STOP ORDER

This is also important, as a trailing stop order is a way of automatically protecting your profits and closing out of a position that you have not been following closely. The trailing stop order is the same as the stop order, except that the price at which the stocks are sold can vary without any intervention on your part.

When you place a trailing stop order, you specify how far down from the maximum price reached you will allow the price to go before the stocks are sold. This is input as a percentage, commonly something like a 5 percent trailing stop. This means that you have a stop order in place for which the value can go up. If your stock doubles in value, the trailing stop will follow it, and if the stock loses value it will be sold when the price drops back down by 5 percent of the highest price reached, so it will become a stop order at 190 percent of the purchase price. Provided the stock rises enough to make the trailing stop as high as your purchase price, then you can only profit on the stock, regardless of whether you ever look at it again.

DAY ORDERS

It is the practice for day traders to close out at the end of each trading day. For this reason, all orders placed are considered to be day orders, unless your broker is notified otherwise. A day order means that the position is not held overnight and the stocks are sold before the markets close for the day (market hours are from 9 a.m.-4 p.m. EST). There is something referred to as after-hours trading, but investors participate in this on an individual basis. Any day orders that are not executed will have to be placed again the next trading day.

GOOD-'TIL-CANCELED ORDERS

You are busy or you will be soon, as you can see by the various types of orders you can place. The last thing you need to be doing is refilling orders that you want to keep going indefinitely. If you want to set a limit price that is different from the market price, a good-'til-canceled order is the type you want to place. Your order will remain in place until it is executed or you cancel it. This allows your order to remain in place for a longer period of time than the average order, even days or weeks, although these orders are still given a limit. Brokerages tend to charge a higher fee for this type of order as well.

CONTINGENT ORDERS

Contingent orders are placed on a contingency basis, the contingency often being that another of your stock holdings is sold before these stocks are bought.

ALL-OR-NONE ORDERS

With all-or-none orders, all stocks requested must be bought according to the original conditions placed in the order. If this is not possible, none of the stocks should be bought and the order should be canceled.

FILL-OR-KILL ORDERS

A fill-or-kill order is a "now or never" order. This type of order must be filled immediately upon placement or it must be killed, which means that it is never filled.

Note that orders can combine some of the various features above — for instance, you may place a limit order and make it good-'til-canceled, or you could make it for the trading day only, when, if unfulfilled, it would just go away.

SELLING SHORT

Selling short is a whole section of the trading spectrum which is ignored by many novice traders, as it is perceived as complicated. Quite simply, when you sell a stock short, you are short of the stock — you have not bought it yet, because you think its value is due to fall and you want to buy it cheaper. This is a way of profiting in a declining market, so it would be useful to learn the basics.

It certainly sounds like a quirky thing to do which you could not achieve in any other branch of business. Look at how the mechanics of selling short work out: in essence, what you are telling your broker to do is to sell a number of shares in the company, and keep the money safe. When you want to realize your profit, you effectively buy the shares at market price, give them to the broker to replace those he sold at the beginning of the trade, and get the money that the broker is holding from the initial sale. Thus, when you buy them more cheaply, you are gaining the difference and profiting from the loss in value of the shares. The price of the shares when you buy to give them back is called the buy-to-cover price, and you are covering your short position when you buy them.

The broker has shares to sell in the first place, when you tell him to because essentially you borrow the shares from the broker, or more likely from one of his clients. This does mean that, rarely, you can be forced to buy the shares at the market price before you want to, when the original owner wants them back and there are no more available. Then, the broker is said to call away the shorted stocks. Because of the way it works, possibly you will not be able to short some stocks, as the market is too limited.

To borrow the shares the broker will charge you the actual cost of the shares at the time of shorting them, plus a commission. Note that if the stocks are due to pay a dividend in the period while you are shorting them, you have to pay the dividend to the original owners — it is only fair, after all, as they would have received it if you had not interfered with their holding. It will also cost you because you must fund the trade from a margin account, which means you may pay interest and other charges associated with this. There will be more about margin accounts later in this chapter.

A potential downside is that there can be unlimited loss

— this is limited only by how high the stock can fly. This is unlike the usual going long (buying the stock directly), when the most you can lose is the current stock value, which you have already paid. This should be an academic problem, as you would be asleep at the wheel if you let the situation get this far — perhaps you should not be a trader at all. As with all trading, as soon as you trade you should create a safety net in the form of a stop order. In this case, it would be called a buy-to-cover stop.

There are some rules that prevent you selling short whenever you want. You are not allowed to short on a stock that is worth less than $5. Neither can you short an IPO (initial public offering). Perhaps of most practical relevance, you cannot short a stock that is going down; you have to wait for an uptick in price. This is a rule developed by the exchanges to prevent too violent a selloff on a failing stock. This rule does not apply to exchange-traded funds (ETFs).

It is interesting to note that shorting a stock guarantees heavy buying in the future. Every short has to be covered at some point, so stocks must be bought. This buying pressure might even support the price of the stock.

Selling short has potential for profit, as long as you study what you are doing. Just consider, when stocks rise they do so in a steady climb. When stocks lose value, the market is not so graceful, as people struggle to unload before the price drops too low. This is an example of fear being a stronger emotion than greed, and it means that there is greater scope for making big gains when you are in the market for shorting stocks. This is an aspect of trading that is well worth a look.

MEET THE BROKERS

Next, you need to know what type of broker you wish to use to execute your trades and build your trading business, and you do need a broker because individuals are not allowed to trade on the exchange without one. Their fees determine the different types of brokers, the types of services they offer, and what they can do for you.

You do need a broker. You cannot trade without one, unless you plan on getting your brokerage license. First, you must decide what type of trading you will be participating in, and then you will be able to judge which services you will need. Then, you will choose your broker based on these criteria. Here is a list of the types of brokers you can choose from and what services they offer.

FULL-SERVICE BROKERS

A full-service broker is just that, a broker who will help you in every way possible. These are the brokers that will often come to you with potential trades to which you can say yes or no. This is because these brokers perform extensive research and offer a variety of services. With full-service brokers, you will pay a transaction fee, and you will also pay a commission based on the amount of the principal. However, you have the whole playing field before you. You are able to trade in stocks, futures, options, bonds, mutual funds, money market funds, and variable annuities. These brokers often have their own Web sites and may allow you to place trades yourself.

You need to be wary of the full-service broker. Get someone

you can trust. Talk to people you know in the trading world and get their advice on who is the best. After all, brokers make their money when you trade, so if there are no transactions they do not get paid. There are some brokers out there who will suggest trades that may not be in your best interest just so that they will get paid. I'm not suggesting that full-service brokers are dishonest, but you need to examine their recommendations to ensure that they are in line with your own ambitions for your account.

If you are to be a success at trading, you must do your own research even if you are using a full-service broker. If your broker was so skilled at picking the stocks to trade, he might make more money trading for himself, rather than facilitating your stock market experience. He undoubtedly has fields of expertise and may be able to give you information of which you were not aware; however, you must be educated and aware of what you are doing with your money. It is about taking responsibility. So often you feel more comfortable passing the blame to others when things go wrong, but in the trading world you cannot claim ignorance. You are the one in charge of your account and your success or failure as a trader. Because you are going to do your own research and you are going to educate yourself, then a full-service broker may offer more than you need. To avoid the extra expense, there are other options.

DISCOUNT BROKERS

The discount broker is exactly that — a broker that costs less money. These brokers offer the same services as a full-service broker, but they do not try to persuade you to pursue certain trades, and they do not offer unsolicited advice. There is no money figured into their fees for them to undertake private research. If you are using a discount broker, you have to know what you are doing and keep yourself well informed.

A simple Internet search for a broker will turn up several companies who will just take your order, online or over the phone, and implement it. You can shop these by price — they range down to about $7 per trade, although you may also get a deal depending on your account balance and amount of trading that you do. The only point to watch is that these brokers may vary in their response time to your order, depending on their setup and staffing. If you are interested mainly in end-of-day trading, you may find that this sort of broker is ideal.

DIRECT-ACCESS BROKERS

Direct-access brokers may be the most flexible type to work with. While you are working through a brokerage, you have direct access to the electronic communications network (ECN) to place your orders and make your trades. You have all Level I NASDAQ quotes, including the latest bid and ask prices, and you also have access to the NASDAQ Level II, which allows you to see everyone who is on the exchange at any given time and what their ask and bid prices are. Using the Level II access, you can always see the real-time best bid and ask prices, which can be extremely helpful when making your trades.

To work with a direct-access broker, you must download

software onto your PC. Because the software is on your PC instead of having to access it through your broker's server, you can trade at a much higher speed. You will not need to wait for pages to download from the server. You are not guaranteed to make all of your trades at the prices you want, but you have a far better chance with a direct-access broker, provided you are hooked up to high-speed Internet.

The software you get through your direct-access broker supplies an abundance of information and raw financial data. You get:

- Actual trades that are happening.

- Current and best bid and ask prices from the different market makers dealing with that stock.

- What the trading volume is at any given time.

- A whole slew of market statistics and tools to help you perform your analysis and determine when and how to trade effectively.

As you develop your own style of trading, you will know how to make this information work for you. Also, with a direct-access broker, the software determines how this information is displayed to you. You can then choose which market or ECN to use when making a trade, which is something that full-service and discount brokers do for you if you work through them.

PROPRIETARY TRADING FIRMS

Proprietary trading firms may be a good option for experienced traders, but they are not for the new trader. These trading firms offer up some of their capital for the trader to use to supplement his trading account. As a trader with a proprietary trading firm, you will share in the profits and may share in the losses, too.

However, you must have a good solid history of trading in the equity markets, and you must have your NASD Series 7 license. You will be expected to learn the trading styles used by the firm, so if you are stuck on the way you trade, then this may not be for you.

FUTURES BROKERS

Futures brokers are brokers that deal strictly with the commodities and futures markets. If you are not working with a full-service broker, then you may need to open an account with one of these brokers if you want to trade in these markets. Having said this, many direct-access brokers provide access to these markets, but you will be hard pressed to find them through a discount broker.

TRADING ON MARGIN

You may have heard the expression, "to trade on margin." Your broker will open a margin account for you, and that gives you access to twice as much money as you originally deposit with him or her. After your money is invested, you can still buy stocks by using your margin, which is the broker's money, lent to you at a good rate of interest (brokers want you to use it and incur transaction fees).

There are strict federal rules about using the margin, or loan money. For instance, it is limited to 50 percent of your account. It is no problem when you start, but if the value of your shareholding slips down, you can find that you need to give the broker more money. For instance, say you deposited $30,000 in your account. That would make $60,000 available to you. If you spent all of this on stocks, and their value sank to $50,000, your money would have sunk to $20,000, and your margin would still be $30,000. This is a problem for two reasons — first, because you used the margin, you have gone into a larger trade than you perhaps should have taken on and lost 33 percent of your money when the stock lost only 17 percent. Second, if your money, or equity, ever sank to a third of the amount you have on margin, the broker would demand more collateral or funds to change the position. This is called a margin call, and it is required by the exchanges if your equity drops to less than 25 percent of your holdings.

When you are selling short, you need to use your margin. For regular trades, however, you want to think carefully about if and when you will go into your margin. It can catch you.

SUCCESS BULLETS

- There are four main types of traders: the scalper (momentum) trader, the day trader, the swing trader, and the position trader.

- The day traders include institutional traders (the specialists and market makers) and retail or individual traders.

- In the market the "inside ask" is the lowest price at which you can buy a stock, and the "inside bid" is the highest price at which you can sell a stock.

- There are two types of analysis: fundamental and technical.

- There are many types of orders you can place: market orders, limit orders, stop orders, stop-limit orders, trailing stop orders, day orders, good-'til-canceled orders, all-or-nothing orders, and fill-or-kill orders.

- Selling short is way to profit by the amount that a stock price falls. It is not available on all stocks. There are limitations in what you can sell short, including that you have to sell short on an uptick in price.

- There are various types of brokers you can work with: full-service brokers, discount brokers, direct-access brokers, proprietary trading firms, and futures brokers.

WORDS TO KNOW

Buy-to-cover, call away, direct-access broker, discount broker, fill, full-service broker, fundamental analysis, Level I/II, limit order, liquidity, long, margin, market order, order, scalper, selling short, slippage, spread, stop, stop order, stop-limit order, trailing stop, uptick

5

MAKE IT YOUR BUSINESS

If you want to trade seriously, whether it is part time or full time, you will need to set yourself up for success. No matter whether you work a full-time job and are planning to trade part time or whether you are planning to jump in with both feet, you had better know where the bottom is, and you had better have a plan. A business plan that is.

You need to set yourself up as a business from day one, and you have to have a business mentality. If you are going to pick away at it, expect to fail — miserably. Knowing how much money you need to start out with and the best setup for your needs will give you the best possible start in the trading world and give you the best chance for success.

GOALS

It is always best to start with the end in mind. It does not seem to matter whether you are writing a book or studying a course on investing or trading; everyone always says to create goals. They are dreams that you have decided will be reality. Make a list of your dreams. Get a piece of paper and write the word "dream" at the top. Then write your dreams down. No matter how grand or how silly they may seem, just write them down. You may have the dream of building your dream home or of moving to Tahiti. You may have the dream of sending your children to the finest universities or colleges, or you may wish to travel the world.

On your list, cross out the word "dreams" at the top of the paper and write "goals" beside it. You have just made your dreams into goals. This means that they are not going to happen "someday." They are not "if only ..." They are tangible goals that you can attain. Just imagine that you have already done them. Imagine you already live in Tahiti. Imagine waking up every morning and seeing the beach outside your house. Feel the ocean breeze coming in your window. Feel the ocean water as you take a morning swim to refresh yourself for the day ahead. Do not just think these things; feel them. Close your eyes and picture them as a reality in your mind. Everything in this world has to be made at least twice: once in someone's mind, then once in reality. You have just set the process in motion by making your goals real once, in your mind. Now all you need is to complete the process and make them real in the world.

As I said in the introduction, every successful endeavor was once a goal. Everything began as a thought. This book was once a thought in someone's mind. The chair you are sitting in, the computer you use every day, and the car sitting in your driveway were all thoughts once upon a time. What happened was that someone took those thoughts, turned them into goals, and made them reality that you can touch and feel.

Do not underestimate the power of your imagination.

You can do many things with it, including becoming a successful trader. Belief in yourself has been trumpeted about for decades, and there is a reason for that. It is the same reason that I am discussing it here. It is because it is necessary for success, life, and wealth.

WHAT KIND OF TRADER ARE YOU?

You have your goals set and written down. You visualize them every day, and you know what you want. Now comes the "how." You need to determine what type of trader you want to be. Do you currently have another "day" job? Do you want to be a full-time or a part-time trader? Regardless of which of these you choose to be, you will need to decide how much risk you are comfortable with and how much money you have with which to open your trading account. If you are a full-time trader, then most likely it is your primary source of income, and as such you will need to ensure that your home office is set up properly, that you have the right computer setup, and that you have researched and chosen your broker well. Here is how you determine whether you qualify as a part-time or a full-time trader:

The part-time trader

- Places three or fewer trades per day and may not trade every day.

- Would rather be a swing or position trader and will contentedly hold onto stocks for days or weeks.

- Wants to be well-informed about the business of

trading but certainly does not want to eat, sleep, and breathe trading.

- Is content to make profits at a slower rate, over a period of time.

The full-time trader

- Trades every day the market is open and places more than three trades per day.

- Makes a plan and makes precision entries and exits.

- Wants to make fast profits and lots of profits.

- Is completely dedicated to understanding the craft and the art of trading and will study daily to achieve that goal.

- Wants to trade for a living.

HARDWARE

Examine the other side of the spectrum. Go from the field of dreams and goals, which begin as thoughts, to the physical hardware needed to make your trading business a true success. You need the proper computer setup to trade effectively, if at all. After all, your computer allows you to research and identify those stocks in which you wish to trade, manage your trading account, and improve your trading.

First, let us talk hardware. You need a good computer. It

is as simple as that. It is preferable that you avoid Apple or Unix/Linux systems if you are purchasing a computer to use specifically for the purpose of trading. A computer with a Windows operating system is more beneficial, as most trading platforms are available for this and use Internet Explorer or similar browser for their display. Here are the minimum hardware requirements to trade effectively:

- **Central Processing Unit (CPU)** — You need a minimum 1.0 GHz processing speed.

- **RAM (Random Access Memory)** — The bottom-line base minimum is 512 MB.

- **Available disk space** — A minimum of 100 MB of free disk space is adequate in the beginning, but you will require more when it comes to the long-term storage of real-time price data.

- **Operating system** — Windows XP at a minimum, or for trading platforms, the most reliable and expensive one you can afford to purchase. Check for compatibility with the software you want to use and for the memory requirement.

- **Video card** — A shared video card (one that shares the RAM) is adequate, but it is by far more beneficial to get a video card that has its own memory with a minimum of 16 MB of memory (32 MB is preferred).

- **Monitor size** — You will potentially be staring at the computer screen all day, so the minimum size should be 17 inches, and oddly enough, LCD is not the best choice, as it can blur moving images; a cathode ray tube (CRT) is better.

- **More than one monitor** — Many traders insist that you need a dual monitor system so that you can use one specifically to look up charts, while the other can be used for everything else. This may depend on what sort of trading you intend to do.

- **Network interface** — Get Ethernet capability.

- **Power supply** — I highly recommend getting an uninterruptible power supply (UPS) so that you are protected in the face of lightning strikes and other power outages. A notebook computer, having a battery built in, is immune to short interruptions in the power supply; however, you will also want to cover any satellite modem or other items. A notebook may not give you the monitor choice that you want, although it is possible to attach external devices.

The next major thing to consider is your Internet access. You must have high-speed access, unless you are sure that you will be trading only at the end of the day. It does not matter if it is DSL or cable-based, but high speed is necessary. In some areas, the only high speed available is from a satellite. This may be more subject to disruption during intense atmospheric activity and storms, but it is still usable. Your entire business and the balance of your trading account may rely on real-time information. That is difficult to obtain when it takes two minutes for data to load through the Internet. Dial-up will not work. If you are a serious and active trader, you may want to consider using a fractional T1 or a dedicated T1 line, but these are expensive. Although this is your primary access, you would be well advised to consider a second means of access to the Internet, even if it is only modem (telephone) based, as this could prevent a total disaster if your first choice of system fails.

If you have a network for connection to other computers, you need to ensure that any wireless connection is secure and password protected. It is difficult to ensure complete security, and you are using it for sensitive personal and financial information. You do not want anyone to gain unauthorized access to your trading account or the information you use when trading.

It is also crucial to your privacy, security, and peace of mind to ensure that you have up-to-date and powerful anti-virus software. Commercially available programs that are widely used include McAfee and Norton. There are also some good free programs, but if you pay for protection you may expect better support. Do not use more than one, as they have been known to interfere with each other and cause problems that are hard to diagnose. I have also had problems trying to switch from one anti-virus program to another, so unless you have a problem with the one you are using, I do not advise changing. Choose one anti-virus program, and be sure that it is set to automatically update. The help available with these products is comprehensive, and you may even be able to run a test to see what areas of your security need attention. They can be configured to give you all the protection that you will need, including spyware and firewall protection.

SOFTWARE

Ticker tape machines are hard to come by these days — and so is replacement ticker tape. It is unusual to find anyone who will spend the time to hand-draw charts; the markets move too quickly for traders to get involved in such matters. Without doubt, computers and access to the Internet have changed the face of trading forever and make it possible for you to compete in the markets on a more equal basis with the professionals. You can order chart books, stock prices, real-time intraday charts, and research reports online and trade in a matter of seconds.

When you start, you are going to use the software provided by your broker to become familiar with the charts and indicators, especially if you are using a direct-access broker. Facilities provided by online broker Web sites can be extensive, and you can learn a great deal from their use and study. This may be the most cost-effective way to start creating charts and analyzing them.

For serious use, you may well graduate to your own software package, such as the widely used industry standard MetaStock. Such packages can be expensive, particularly if you purchase or subscribe to additional services and features. However, for a full-time trader there are also tremendous benefits from such a package, not least of which is a terrific user group, which means that you will not be wasting time discovering how to do what you want — someone is bound to have done it already and be ready to talk about it.

Read David Jenyns story below — a successful trader and teacher, he uses MetaStock.

SUCCESS STORY: DAVID JENYNS

David Jenyns is recognized as a leading expert on designing profitable trading systems. He earned this title after working at one of Australia's top brokerage firms, Ord Minnett.

To date David has written numerous best-selling trading books and courses including, *The MetaStock Programming Study Guide* book, The MetaStock Secrets Seminar DVD, "Trading Secrets Revealed" audio guide, and *Ultimate Trading Systems* book. He has also been published in trade magazines, including *Chartpoint, Your Trading Edge*, and *The Guppy Traders Newsletter*.

David now trades professionally, actively runs seminars and one-on-one training, and plans out systematic moneymaking trading systems. To download a free copy of David's trading system, visit **www.freetradingsystems.org**.

What types of trading are you involved with?	I trade using a system based on the Nicholas Darvas box trading method. This is a momentum trading system that effectively rides medium to long-term trends. I have added a few tweaks to make sure the system suits my personality and trading style; however, the fundamentals of the system are the same. The core of the system is based on identifying strongly performing stocks making new highs, purchasing on strengths, and then riding the trend until it ends. The method could be termed medium to long term (anywhere from two to three months to 12 months) depending on how long the trend continues, and I trade this method on medium to large-cap stocks within the Australian market. In addition to the Darvas method, I also write covered calls over the underlying stocks to further magnify my trading profits.
How did you start trading?	I first got introduced to the markets through a friend at high school. He was trading during the early days of the Internet boom and would come to school and tell me how much money he'd made. I was amazed that he could manage his trading while still at school — just trading at home and breaks between classes. This really inspired me, and as a result, at the completion of my studies, I took out a $5,000 loan to start a share-trading course. I think I was luckily at the right place at the right time, since at

SUCCESS STORY: DAVID JENYNS	
	the completion of the course the Internet boom was just building momentum.
	I invested what little money I had and almost immediately got a taste of success.
What were your main concerns when starting trading?	Perhaps the biggest concern was that I did not have enough capital to trade. I'd just taken out the $5,000 loan for my share-trading course, and that meant that I had very little money to trade with. I was very cautious and mindful of the fact that if I lost my trading capital I would not be able to trade.
	I found myself really focusing on preserving my capital. I think this positioned me well for the rest of my trading career. I now approach the market with a similar manner regardless of how much capital I have … my number one concern is to protect what I have.
How soon did you see a steady flow of income?	Having just invested a considerable amount of money in my education, I really did not have much of a trading float when I started. Unfortunately, when you are investing with a very small amount of capital, it is easy for it to be eroded away by brokerage.
	I found that for the first 12 months, while I was still learning, I was really only treading water, or marginally in front. That said, I saw this as success since most people lose money when they first start trading the market … and moreover, I was trading with very little capital.
	I realized that there is a huge advantage to having a larger trading float once you have got the methodology down … and it really does make trading easier. For this reason I decided to take a break from trading and build up my trading float.
	I started working for Ord Minnett, a large stockbroking firm in Australia, using the time with them to further my studies and build up my trading float. Within 12 months I was back trading the markets with much greater success. All considered, it really took about two years before I became profitable.

SUCCESS STORY: DAVID JENYNS

| What are your likes and dislikes about trading? | Obviously I'm a little biased in that I think trading is one of the most profitable and advantageous financial endeavors you can undertake. That said, I suppose there are some drawbacks to trading.

First, trading can be time consuming if you do not have the right system and method in place. Second, I do not like the solitary nature of trading. I'm a social person who enjoys the company of others. When you are trading at home, unless you have a support network, you can become quite isolated.

The final and my most prominent dislike about trading is … making losses. Sure I understand it is part of trading; every successful trading system will have losses. Nevertheless, that still does not take away from the fact that I do not like trading losses!

Now for the good stuff … there are so many things to like about trading.

First, you can do it anywhere. You are not restricted geographically to any one region, particularly with the advent of the Internet. The way information flows so freely means that no matter where you are, you can trade the markets.

Another fantastic thing about trading is that once you have defined your actual methodology, there is the potential to automate it. You could even take automation to the next level and hire someone to trade your systems for you — thereby fully automating your system.

Last, but not least, my favorite thing about trading is the fact that it provides a huge amount of leverage. Leverage in both time and money. Once you have automated your trading system, the time input required can be quite minimal, yet the rewards can be disproportionately large. In addition, you also get leverage of your money working very hard for you … you even have the ability to borrow and let other people's money work hard for you too.

I really believe trading is the perfect business! |

SUCCESS STORY: DAVID JENYNS

What personal qualities helped you to become a trader?	Perhaps the most important quality was my hunger and desire to master the art and craft of trading. I made a decision early on that I was going to be the very best trader I could be using my chosen trading method.
	I decided that I was going to do whatever it took to become a profitable trader.
	Another great skill is my ability to model others achieving success. I believe the ability to almost copycat already successful traders and their trading methods shortcut a lot of wasted time and energy for me. Sure, you need to tailor any trading system to your own needs, but it is much easier to tailor an already successful system than create one from scratch.
	Perhaps the most important quality would be discipline. Discipline in the early days to do what needs to be done when designing a profitable trading system. There is a process for designing trading systems, and most traders simply do not have the discipline to follow this mythology.
	Even to this day discipline is a fundamental quality that can be attributed to my success. It enables me to trade my system, as defined in my trading plan, without a second thought. I let my system do the work … so I do not have to.
What is the biggest challenge you have faced in trading?	The biggest challenge I have faced in trading is to take a big loss when it needs to be taken. I touched on this earlier, that all trading systems produce losing trades, but that never makes it any easier.
	With that said, I know from experience that all huge losses once started out with small losses. I will always prefer to exit with a small loss and avoid a potentially devastating trade.
What advice would you give potential traders?	Design a trading plan that matches your objectives and temperament. Most traders focus on potential rewards and markets that are currently "fashionable." They fail to identify what their personal objectives are first.
	You need to take note of things like:

SUCCESS STORY: DAVID JENYNS

	• How much time do you have to commit to the market?
	• How much money will you be trading with?
	• Are you looking for an income or capital growth?
	• What is your level of risk tolerance?
	By not defining these first, most traders end up trading a market or a system that will never achieve their objectives. It is for this reason I advise that would-be traders design a trading system that suits them, and do not buy a black-box trading system.
	You need to know what it is you are trading and why it is you are trading that methodology.
What qualities do you think are important in a would-be trader?	When a new trader first comes to the market, it is extremely important that they have a thirst to learn. Many would-be traders come to the market with the unrealistic expectation that they will return a huge profit with very little time and/or capital input.
	I believe would-be traders with a thirst to learn stand a much better chance of success because they are more likely to go through the process that is required to design a profitable trading system. They will take the time to do the due diligence and appropriate groundwork.
	That said, you need a balance between learning and taking action. Many people find that their thirst to learn is too strong, and without an action-orientated personality, they get stuck in the cycle of information consumption.
	I think a lot can be learned by trading the market, because the market really is the best teacher of trading. So, once the appropriate amount of learning has been done, action needs to be taken to implement your trading system.
	And, last but definitely not least, is the quality of discipline. To be successful in trading you need discipline... no two buts about it. You need discipline to follow your trading plan and to do what needs to be done when it needs to be done regardless of how emotionally involved you may be.

SUCCESS STORY: DAVID JENYNS	
When did you know that you would be successful?	I have always known that I was going to be successful, and this was never limited to trading the markets. I have always have had a feeling that no matter what I do, I will be successful at it. A big part of this confidence stems from the fact that when I look at other people who have achieved success in various fields, they do not appear to have any real advantage over myself. They may have simply studied longer than I have at their chosen field, but with enough time I feel I can get myself up to speed. In fact, before starting any endeavor I make the resolve that I will be successful ... I leave no room for any other outcome. With trading I found an already successful trading method, adapted it to suit my personality, and became the best trader I could using my chosen method. Material success soon followed.
Describe your typical day.	When trading the markets, I start the day by reviewing what happened from the night before in overseas markets (particularly the U.S.). Next, before the market opens, I look at all my current open positions and recalculate their trading stop-losses to ensure they are set appropriately. If there are any changes, these are entered into my trading platform. I like to use automated exits, where if my stop-loss is breached I'm immediately taken out of the trade. I usually watch the market open for the first 30 minutes of the day to get a general feel of how the market is reacting to overnight trading ... and with that, the majority of the day is actually spent working on other wealth-creation endeavors. I do not spend hours of the day staring at the screen; I let my system do the work. During the last 30 minutes of the trading day I take an intraday snapshot of the market action and scan the market for any new potential trading opportunities. I enter accordingly if my system says there are any new trading candidates. I think many new traders do themselves a disservice if they spend the entire day staring at the screen, watching every stock movement. It is much easier to get an itchy trigger finger when

	SUCCESS STORY: DAVID JENYNS
	you spend all day watching the markets, and this causes over-trading — a big source of failure in the markets. If you have already put the hard work into designing a trading system, you then need to let your system work for you. For me, I find the easiest way to let my system do the work is to focus on other things while the market is trading.
What is the biggest trading mistake you ever made?	The biggest trading mistake I ever made was when I first started trading CFDs (contract for difference). I tried to trade a system that I had designed for another market on CFDs, thinking it would simply multiple its profits, as CFDs are a leveraged product. Unfortunately, this particular trading system had quite large stops. This worked fine with unleveraged instruments because the risk was minimized. However, the size of the loss, when calculated out using the CFD leverage, was a considerably larger level of risk than I was comfortable with. Nevertheless, I started to trade this system and only realized the hard way that the system was not suited to the type of instrument I was trading. I had based my stops on the underlying instrument with no consideration given to the leverage involved. It just so happened that my first trade was a losing one, and the result was when I did finally get stopped out, the loss far exceeded my maximum risk. I learned a very valuable lesson. Your system must match the market you are trading. What is more, if you make a mistake it is much better to immediately close out the position and re-evaluate, rather than holding on to see what happens.
Which stock indicator do you pay the most attention to?	Being a trend-following trader, my favorite indicator is the "Highest High" function. This is a function within my charting package MetaStock. Using this I am easily able to identify stocks trading at or very near to their 12-month high. It makes it super easy to spot currently trending stocks where I can continue to ride the trend.

SUCCESS STORY: DAVID JENYNS	
Describe your setup of computer, software, and Internet connection.	I'm currently running three computers. That said, I do most of my analysis on the desktop — the laptops are more for while I'm on the road. They are pretty stock standard computers running Windows XP. My Internet connection is just a DSL line. I only have a few tools and software programs loaded on these computers. I use MetaStock as my charting package, and I get my data from a provider called Premium Data. Together these tools help me scan the market for profitable trading opportunities. Lastly, my broker has a platform which gives me access to market depth and gives me the ability to place my trades and set stops online.

As part of a software subscription or as a separate subscription, you need to have the market data available in a suitable format. You should expect to spend at least $60 per month for good services, but the software you use is going to supply you with all of the tools necessary to prosper in your online trading business. The software should allow for:

- Market research

- Charting capabilities

- Streaming prices

- News services

Ideally, you will want a trading platform that is up to date and ready for expansion in the future. As you go along in your trading career you will develop your own strategies. After all, trading is an individual and personal thing. Ultimately, you may need access to the following tools:

Trading tools include:

- Stock trading

- Option trading strategies and support

- Futures trading

- NASDAQ Level II access

- Direct-access trading and ECN book data

- Automatic notifications

- Watch lists

Analysis tools include:

- Sector analysis

- Analysts reports

- Time and volume sales reports

- News feeds

- Real-time charting capabilities

Account management tools include:

- Real-time account balances

- Real-time updates of buying power and margin exposure

- Open-order status

- Portfolio management tools

YOUR TRADING ENVIRONMENT

You have two choices when it comes to your trading platform or trading environment. You can either go with browser-based trading or use an integrated trading platform. As a novice trader, you may be safe enough sticking with browser-based trading because you may not be trading in high volumes of stock yet and will not be needing the speed of the platform. The integrated platform is better for higher volume and intraday trading.

BROWSER-BASED TRADING

A browser-based trading environment can be supported by any computer and any browser software, although Windows-based computers are the most popular. Your broker will provide any software required, and you will want to confirm the level of integration and the capabilities of the software. Sometimes this software is integrated, and sometimes it is fairly basic and fragmented in what it offers and how it performs. Some brokers make it easy to use the software, and some do not. If you cannot find information that you want or need through this trading environment, you can find it elsewhere on the Internet for no cost or a low cost.

On the flip side, these trading applications can be slow and can require you to open multiple browser windows simultaneously. You may have to perform many tasks or enter much information and commands manually, depending on how your broker has set up the system. You also may find that, depending on the browser, you may have issues with your Internet connection if your screen is not active for a time. Again, if you are a new or low-volume trader these things will not affect your trading business to any great extent.

INTEGRATED TRADING PLATFORM

An integrated trading platform is a definite advantage if you are going to be trading in high volume or if you are a day trader and you are counting on speed. Integrated systems are faster, and they are more user-friendly. These systems are ideal for those traders who want to develop their own trading system and bypass the browser-based systems.

Some of these systems are basic, but some of them are so sophisticated that you are trading on an institutional trading level. This means you can program hot buttons to make trading faster and enter multiple orders for different stocks at the same time. You will be able to fine-tune your personal trading strategies with many of these systems, and you will have incredible support.

Having said all of this, these systems are costly, and your broker may charge more if you are using one of them. You may have to maintain a high account balance, or you may need to commit to a minimum number of trades per month. They want guaranteed volume. However, if you are a full-time day trader, then you may find this is worth the extra cost. You absolutely must have the best hardware capabilities if you plan to use an integrated trading platform.

SUCCESS BULLETS

- You must have clear goals of where you want to go and what you want to accomplish. Goals are merely dreams with a schedule. Write them down.

- Determine if you are a part-time trader or a full-time trader. What do you want out of your trading business, and how much do you want to put into it?

- You have to ensure that you have a computer system and a high-speed Internet connection to be able to play the trading game. Your system requirements must be top of the line, especially if you are going to trade in high volume or if you are going to be a day trader.

- You need to research your software options and what your broker can offer you. If you are a low-volume trader, web browser-based trading will suffice. If you are a high-volume trader, you will likely need an integrated trading platform.

WORDS TO KNOW

Browser-based, CFD, integrated trading platform

6

How Will You Trade?

There are two ways to trade on the market. You can use an online broker, or you can go it alone with a direct-access trading platform. If you are using a broker, you simply call your broker or send the order to tell him that you want X number of shares. When your broker receives your order, he will then electronically submit that trade to a specialist or market maker at the appropriate exchange. When the order is filled, your broker will receive notification of your order with the details of how many shares were bought and at what price. He will then send you confirmation. This all happens within seconds to minutes.

If you choose to use a direct-access platform, you will simply send the order through yourself. It will go from you directly to the specialist or market maker, and you will receive immediate confirmation that your order was filled and the terms upon which it was filled. Both of these options were discussed in detail in Chapter 4.

THE TRADING RULE BOOK

In trading there are rules to follow, and most of them are government-regulated rules. However, your broker may have more strict rules than those imposed by government legislation. You need to be sure you know whose rules you need to follow and what they are.

MARGIN REQUIREMENTS

Margin requirements are a government rule. The Federal Reserve's Regulation T stipulates that traders may borrow up to a maximum of 50 percent of the cost of the shares. For instance, if you open your trading account with $15,000, your broker can then lend you another $15,000. This is not free money. If you use it, and I do not recommend that you do unless absolutely necessary, you will pay interest on this loan.

Now say you do use this money, along with your own, and you purchase $30,000 worth of stock. You then have an account balance of $0, an equity balance of $15,000, and a margin balance of $15,000. If the stock price increases, your equity increases and you are secure. You can even use this equity to borrow more margin money if you wish. However, if the stock price falls, you will end up with a lower equity balance while the margin balance remains the same. So, say your equity balance is now $10,000 and your margin balance is still $15,000. You are allowed to purchase only 50 percent of your stocks with your margin account, and in this case, $15,000 is now more than 50 percent. You will have to either deposit more money into the account or sell some of the shares. This is a good way to lose some control of how you are trading.

The NYSE and NASD also have regulations. You are not to

allow the equity in your account to fall below 25 percent of the total balance of the account. If it does your broker will demand you provide additional money or collateral to support the margin loan. This is what is known as a margin call. You either need to deposit cash or fully paid, un-margined securities from another trading account. If you do not do this, your broker is allowed to sell as much as four times the amount of stock necessary to pay off the margin call, and this can be any stock from your portfolio. This means you can lose money.

The recommended thing to do in a situation like this is to close the position that has resulted in the margin call. You can end up owing more than you borrowed with your margin account, and you can lose more money than you originally deposited. You should also know that not all stocks can be bought on margin, and not all stocks can be used as collateral.

SETTLING TRADES

When you buy stock, you must pay for that stock within three business days. When selling stock, your money is most likely being held in the brokerage account and will be released within three days as well. This money will be available to cover any stock purchases.

FREE RIDING

When you are free riding, it means that you are selling a stock before you have paid for it. This is possible because of the three-day period you have to settle the purchase deal.

You can buy stock and turn around and sell it without having paid for it yet. Many traders are margin traders, which means that they use their margin account to trade. They are able to use the money that they have committed to the unsettled trade to borrow more until the trade is settled. This is an official rule with the Federal Reserve's Regulation T, which states that a brokerage firm may buy or sell a security on your behalf if either:

- You have sufficient funds in your account.

- The brokerage firm accepts in good faith your commitment to pay in full and in cash the balance owing on the security before you sell it.

If you do go for a free ride and you do not have the account balance to cover the purchase, your broker can freeze your account for 90 days. During this time period, if you wish to make any purchases, you must pay for them that day, as you have lost the three-day settlement period.

YOUR TRADING ACCOUNT

Toni Turner, in her book *A Beginner's Guide to Day Trading Online*, warns against trading with "scared money." This means that you should trade only with money you can afford to lose. To use any other money, even on a "sure thing," is dicey and could have dire consequences and possible bankruptcy. She is absolutely right. If you lose the money in your trading account, what will happen? Will you lose your house? Will you go bankrupt? Or do you just say, "Well, maybe trading was not for me," and move on to bigger and better things? You need to think this through carefully.

The money in your trading account must be separate from the money you need in your day-to-day life. If it is not, it is going to breed fear, and fear is one of the dreaded emotions that can rule a trade and cause you to lose money. Trading with "scared money" makes you do stupid things. You can make poor decisions, and your fear can entice greed to join the party. This is when things can go wrong. Sure, there may be times in which you will get lucky and your greed will allow you to profit, but chances are, more often than not, you will lose out to greed.

You may decide to open two trading accounts. Turner discusses this option in her book. The idea behind this is that you have one account that is a direct-access account that is specifically for day trading and one that is in place with an online broker for longer-term trading, such as position trading. There are four good reasons for having two accounts:

1. You will most likely be able to place stop-limit and good-'til-canceled orders on your trades using the account with the online broker. This way, when you take a day off, you do not have to worry about your account.

2. You will be able to avoid using your margin when you make a mistake and use a margin call. You have a margin in your trading account that is 50 percent your account. This margin is a loan from your broker that is matched with the deposit you put into the account when you opened it. If you use this money, they will charge interest on it, so you do not want to max out your account. Consider this margin

emergency money. When you accidentally (or not) place an order that goes into your margin, you will often get a warning from your broker, but sometimes this does not happen. You can use the money in your second account to cover the margin call.

3. If your broker's server goes down, you could be in big trouble, especially if you need to get out of a position quickly. You can go to your other account (it needs to be with a different broker) and hedge your first account from there.

4. When you are a new trader (or if you are not) and losing money most days, you can often find relief when you look at your second account and see it making money, as it is often easier to make money in the beginning when position trading.

SUCCESS BULLETS

- You can trade through an online broker, or a direct-access platform allows you to place trades directly.

- Federal regulations limit your use of the "margin" that your broker will place at your disposal.

- It may take three days to settle a trade, to pay or receive money.

- Free riding is selling shares before you have even paid for them.

- You must keep a minimum balance in your trading account if you are day trading.

- Having a second trading account with an online broker for your longer-term trades is recommended.

WORDS TO KNOW

Free riding, margin call

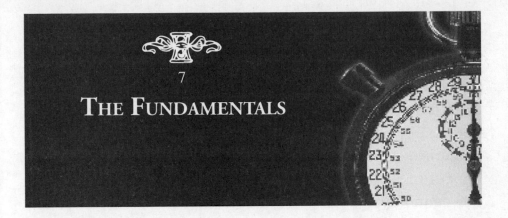

7

THE FUNDAMENTALS

When it comes down to it, the stock market is heavily intertwined with the economy. The markets rise and fall in relationship with the economy, as well as other external influences. Therefore, to be an investor that relies on fundamental analysis, you must understand the basics of how the economy works. In your lifetime, you will have noticed that the economy goes through natural cycles, ups and downs, periods of growth and recession. Whenever you hear the word recession you cringe and brace yourself for the blow. Well, if you trade in the long term, more correctly termed investing, with some of your portfolio, you do not just brace yourself; you run for the bomb shelters and hope to get away with the clothes on your back and, if you are lucky, with your trading portfolio and account at least somewhat intact. If you see it coming, you should make drastic changes in your position and get out of shares and into money instruments checks, bills, money orders, Certificates of Deposit, etc.).

Just like market trends, the business cycle of the economy goes up and comes down. When it is up, people are happy and filling their pockets, but it has to come down at some point. Those who are ready for it make off relatively unscathed, and some may even profit from the misfortunes of others. However, many people do not fare as well. The Board of Governors of the Federal Reserve (Fed) is responsible for changes in the monetary policy in the United States, and the government is responsible for any tax changes and any fiscal policy changes. Together, these two groups can have some influence on and minimize the impact of the highs and lows of inflation and recession in the economy, but they cannot eradicate them. After all, what goes up must come down, and the higher it goes the faster and farther it falls.

Many people believe that the government can save all crises. The truth is that Fed Chairman Ben Bernanke is limited in what he can do, and sometimes there is no easy answer. Take for instance the sub-prime mortgage crisis, current at the time of this writing. The dollar is weak and getting weaker, as there is a deepening trade deficit; the American consumers are hurting, as the cost of borrowing money rises. To make the dollar more attractive to overseas investors, and thus bolster its value, you need a higher interest rate; to ease the consumers' problems, you need a lower interest rate. The Fed's answer is to lower the interest rate. This keeps the U.S. consumer spending, mostly on imports, which keeps the global economy moving. It keeps the people happy in the runup to the election. The reduction in interest rates also stimulates the U.S. economy, as U.S. goods are cheaper to export. Thus the stock market can be expected to keep rising; all the while, the greenback buys less in the world, and the real wealth of the average American is slashed.

As a trader, your goal is not to become an expert on a particular company or an economist. Instead, you need to understand the underlying trends that move the economy. Fundamental analysis helps in understanding how long trends may last, but the stock market is not synchronized with the economy — by their nature, the prices of stocks are forward looking and reflect the future as understood by the investors. It is not the current position. Often, you will find when quarterly results are announced that the stock price does not go in the obvious direction, as the market had already anticipated the results and factored them into the current price. Say IBM had a bad quarter. When it is announced, you may well find that the stock price does not go down; the cognoscenti and those on the inside track knew enough beforehand that the price had already declined, if appropriate. You may even find the price increasing, as a result of the results being confirmed and no worse than thought.

THE ECONOMY

Fundamental analysis can be viewed at three levels, from the top down. First, the economy must be understood. Each month a series of reports are issued by the government and other agencies which comment on various aspects of the economy. Some are weekly reports, and some are issued monthly. The most important ones to us are considered next.

Employment Situation

The Bureau of Labor Statistics issues a report on the first Friday of each month. The essential elements include:

- Payrolls (non-farm), which provide a measure of the number of jobs created.

- Unemployment rate, which compares the number of unemployed people to the total labor force.

- Average work week, which measures the total hours worked.

- Average hourly earnings, the wages earned.

From this report you get an idea of how healthy the labor market is. A healthy market indicates a growing economy and company profits. Unemployment rises during downturns and falls during economic growth.

Consumer Price Index (CPI)

The consumer price index is also issued once a month, along with the similar producer price index (PPI). These indexes provide some measure of the rise in the cost of living on a retail and on a wholesale basis, although recent objections have pointed out important discrepancies between the CPI and the real spending of a typical consumer. In the early 1990s, there was much talk that inflation was overstated, and the method of calculating the CPI was changed. Recent objections assert that the current methods understate inflation and provide a measure not for keeping a constant standard of living but for a declining standard of living.

Also more recently, the effect of the CPI on stocks has been declining, but it is still invoked in wage negotiations as well as used for Social Security increases, so an increase in CPI would cause the Fed to tighten monetary policy and stifle growth and profitability.

Gross Domestic Product (GDP)

The GDP is due out quarterly, but there are updates issued, so it seems to come out every month. It does have an effect on stock prices. Economists tend to think that the optimum rate of growth of the GDP is about three and one-half percent, to avoid inflationary pressures. If it is higher than this, the market tends to anticipate that the Fed will have to step in with increased interest rates to slow things down.

Federal Open Market Committee (FOMC)

Speaking of the Fed, the Federal Open Market Committee (FOMC) meets at least eight times a year to determine if there is a need to adjust monetary policy. The main result is to adjust the short-term interest rates as the committee thinks necessary.

THE MARKET SECTOR

The market sector that a company is in counts toward how good an investment it can be. A terrific company in a depressed sector may be a less good investment than an average company in a good sector.

There are four stages to the business cycle. These are:

1. **Peak:** When the economy is at its peak, everyone is happy. The Gross Domestic Product (GDP) is near its maximum output. Employment is up so people have jobs and income is increasing. Of

course, when income increases, so do prices, and inflation is looming overhead. This is a time of prosperity.

2. **Recession:** The economy cannot remain at its peak forever. The transition from its peak to its trough is called the recession, and when it begins to fall, so do employment levels. Income and prices level off, and production output dies down. If the recession is long, income and prices will begin to fall.

3. **Trough:** This is the opposite of the peak. The recession will bottom out and the economy will begin to stabilize. This is where depression can set in, if the trough lasts for a long time. The economy and the people wait for the recovery.

4. **Expansion/Recovery:** This is the transition from the trough to the peak. It is during this time that the economy is bouncing back and things are beginning to look up again. Once again, employment, income, and production are increasing, and the next peak is on its way. This is a good time to be correctly placed in the stock markets.

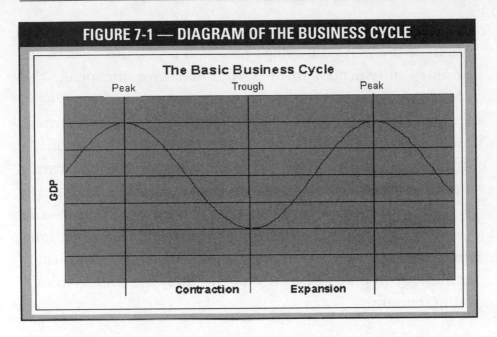

FIGURE 7-1 — DIAGRAM OF THE BUSINESS CYCLE

The National Bureau of Economic Research (NBER) is the official tracker of the business cycle in the United States. NBER tracks the peaks and troughs and notifies the private and public sectors when the economy is going into a recession or an expansion. You can find it at **www.nber. org**. Unfortunately, this information is not given in real time. You do not find out what part of the business cycle you have been in until you are well into it or it has already passed. In other words, this is no early warning system. The collection and processing of all of this economic data takes time, and NBER will make no official announcements until it can back its words up with solid research.

The business cycle affects the individual market sectors differently. Some sectors perform better in certain stages of the cycle, and if you feel that you can discern the stage of the cycle that the economy is in, you have a quick reference to what markets to look at.

Here is a guide to the sectors that relate to the stages of the business cycle. As the cycle reaches a peak, the healthcare industry is expected to do well. Just over the peak, the stocks of consumer staples such as food and beverages perform well and continue fairly strongly, as consumers find ways to pay for these even when going into recession. At the trough, financial stocks such as banks and insurance companies tend to be better than the market, and again they continue to do well as conditions improve. As the recovery takes hold, technology and telecommunications may lead the way, as businesses attempt to update their technology to take advantage of the upswing and to match rising demand.

THE COMPANIES

Now that you understand how the economy fluctuates and moves throughout time, you can examine how a particular market sector responds to this outside pressure. Supply and demand, which was discussed in detail earlier, fluctuate with the economy. Anything that affects supply and demand is considered a fundamental of the market. For instance, weather and seasonal influences will determine the state of affairs for natural gas stocks. In the winter, usage or demand goes up, and so do the prices.

Within the sector, you will have companies that perform well and others that are not so good. The sector is represented by the average performance, and companies vary from this to a greater or lesser extent. Any particular company's financial well-being will be the basis for the fundamental analysis necessary to make wise trading and investment decisions. The company information most examined includes the stock's annual growth rate, the company's quarterly earnings, as well as the earnings over a one-year and five-year period, and its P/E (price-to-earnings) ratios. You should also review the market share of the company among its peers to see if it is well placed to take advantage of any sector growth.

Company fundamentals are the basis of stock fundamental analysis. Arguably, the value of a share represents its future worth, and this is sometimes called "present value" by economists. You may be familiar with the concept of the present value of money; for instance, if you decide you want $20,000 in five years to buy a new car, you can work out what amount (present value) you need to put in an account today at a certain rate of interest to achieve that. In relation to shares, you can determine the present value by a process called "discounting," effectively saying that an amount in the future is worth only a lesser, or discounted amount today.

For dividend-paying shares, you can simply figure that the price is worth the discounted stream of dividends you can expect if you hold on to the stock forever. If the stock does not pay a dividend a the moment, you must assume a certain value in the future when you sell it, and today's price should be the discounted value of that. This can become a circular argument, so is not easily implemented.

The alternative approach that value investors use is to look at the company's stream of earnings, as opposed to a stream of dividends — the argument being that the company's earnings are or will become dividend payouts ultimately. In the meantime, the earnings pay off the company's debts, or grow the company, both of which are increasing the value anyway. This leads to a shortcut in valuing the stocks — looking at the price/earnings ratio (P/E). This is the stock price per share, divided by the earnings per share, for the past year.

In and of itself, the P/E does not prove anything, but it can be compared to other companies in the market sector, to previous years' figures, and to the market as a whole. It is so easy to find that it is a leading indicator for investors. A high P/E might indicate that a company is overvalued, just as a low P/E may indicate that the stock is undervalued and a good buy — but a low P/E may also indicate that the company is in trouble, despite its earnings, and that market watchers have realized that. The typical range of P/E for the market as a whole is about 15 to 25 and varies with the market sector.

There is a further refinement on the same lines as the P/E, and that is the PEG ratio. This is the P/E ratio divided by the percent expected annual earnings growth rate. If the PEG is low, it is expected that the stock is undervalued (growth is high, relative to P/E). Companies that have a high P/E are thus vindicated if they also have a high growth rate, as in the high-tech boom. The Motley Fool investment advice recommends buying stocks with a PEG of 0.5 or less and selling with a PEG of 1.5 or more.

The traders and investors who are looking at fundamental analysis are interested in the year-to-year market behavior of a specific stock rather than the daily and weekly performance. The economist Robert Shiller has long argued, with some truth, that the fundamentals of a stock do not change nearly as much as its price, but, as long as the stocks have shown a steady rise over a long period of time, investors are content to wait it out and watch their profits grow.

Position traders, many commodities brokers, and some traders rely on fundamentals. Many technical analysts will scoff at fundamentals, but the truth is this information is incredibly useful. If you are planning to hold on to the shares longer for than a day trader, you may want to know that the company is a sound one. One major reason more traders do not rely on fundamentals is because of the time involved in doing the research. When you are staring at five-minute charts all day while keeping an eye on volume and various indicators as well as CNBC, you have no time left over for fundamentals. However, doing your fundamentals research can put you one move ahead of the other players in the trading game.

THE METHOD TO AVOID THE MADNESS

When you want to choose a company in which to invest, you must first start with the industry or sector. You should check out the supply and demand for the services or products involved before deciding on the sector. Once you have an idea of where you wish to begin in relation to the big picture, you can then narrow it down and pick out a few companies (at least two) that are in a similar business. From here you can compare and decide which would be the best investment. For each company, you will need to review and analyze the company reports, which will contain some of the other information you require. For instance, the profit and loss statement is a basic factor that will show you the company's trading health.

Other factors, which you can easily look up, are the P/E ratios, the market share, earnings growth, and the sales figures. Looking at the historic factors will give you a comparison to see how the company is faring against previous years, and looking at other companies in the sector will give a direct comparison of the fundamental values.

THE ANALYST

Analysts are people who have been raised to the status of prophet in the trading world. They can be useful, but their advice should always be approached with caution, as there may be some vested interests. You must be wary of the analyst and make sure you find an honest one. There have been many scandals in the recent past that have shown the true nature of many of these analysts. They often get their information via conference calls that are sponsored by the companies when they report their earnings and make financial announcements. We are now in a time when individual investors and traders can listen in on these calls.

When you are considering an analyst, do know whom he or she represents and what type of analyst he or she is. These are truly important questions, because if analysts do not give you accurate information and you buy stocks on their recommendations, you could be in for a big surprise. After all, you have to know and remember that these people are getting their paycheck from the brokerages and the institutions that they represent. Here are the different types of analysts, which should give you a feel for what each one represents and what may be in it for him or her to promote certain stocks to you.

Buy-side Analysts

These are the analysts you hear but do not see. They are the analysts who work for the large firms, the institutional investment firms that manage mutual funds or maintain and manage private accounts. Their primary role is to analyze the stocks bought by the company, not the ones bought by the individual investor. People outside of the institution do not get to see the analysis, as this information is gathered primarily for the company to ensure that a particular investment will fit in with its investment strategy and portfolio. These analysts often include information gleaned from the sell-side analysts.

Sell-side Analysts

Sell-side analysts can cause much conflict in the trading and investment world. They represent the brokerage firms and other financial distribution companies that are in business to sell to the individual trader and investor. The firm, not the individual, pays them, so you need to know whether the recommendations based on their reports are of benefit to you as well as the firm (they are always of benefit to the firm, otherwise the analyst would not get a paycheck). In other words, you need to make sure the analysts' reports and recommendations represent the interests of all the players, because yours will not be at the top of the list.

There was a time when the analysts worked independently from the investment business side of the wall. They were not aware of the deals being made and vice versa. Unfortunately, the wall came down and analysts were included in the fundamentals of deals and mergers that were being made. Of course, their reports supported their side of the coin, and small investors were at risk. There have since been reforms put in place that help investors identify potential conflicts of interest so that they can protect their interests.

Independent Analysts

Independent analysts are the analysts you can trust the most. They are a mysterious breed, and they work for wealthy individuals or institutional investors. They may work only with those people who maintain large portfolios of more than a million dollars, and they are paid incredible fees. With the requirement for independent research on the rise, these are the analysts of the future. You can often access these analysts through your brokerage house or investment research firms for a lower cost than you would pay to the analyst himself. Are they truly independent? Maybe, maybe not. Someone pays them the majority of their money and that person likely is not you, but they are your safest bet when considering the help of an analyst.

Analysts are particularly useful for providing historical data on a company or what an industry is doing. When you get a report from an analyst, you are looking at five years' worth of data, although you can go back further if you wish. The analysts will then make predictions about a company's or industry's earning potential based on their research that might be useful in your decision-making process.

You should note that fundamentals are only half of the story. It is not possible to trade on the basis of fundamentals alone, and that is why the rest of this book will focus on technical analysis and the short-term movements of stock prices.

SUCCESS BULLETS

- The economy goes through four cycles, the peak, recession, the trough, and recovery.

- The federal government has a certain but limited ability to change the course of the economy.

- Companies also go through cycles similar to the economy.

- The direction of stock prices does not always follow obvious paths — the prices reflect future expectations, not current circumstances.

- The status of the economy is gauged by regular reports from the government and others; these include the unemployment figures, the consumer price index, and the gross domestic product.

- Companies should be selected by starting with the business sector and looking at the fundamentals.

- Company fundamentals, such as company debt, income and expenditures, and dividends paid, are the basis of fundamental analysis.

- The P/E and the PEG are measures of a company's strength but may be misleading.

- Buy-side analysts work for institutions, and it is unlikely that you will have access to their findings.

- Sell-side analysts often work for brokers, and their advice may be available to you, but they are paid by the brokers and may not have your best interests at heart.

- You may be able to pay for research by independent analysts by subscribing to newsletters. This may not be their main source of income, however, which can color their reports.

- You must be cautious in trusting analysts' findings, as they may not have your best interests at heart.

WORDS TO KNOW

Buy-side analyst, dividend, gross domestic product, P/E, sell-side analyst

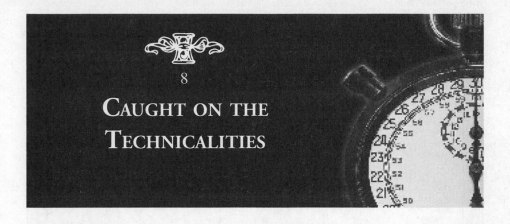

8

CAUGHT ON THE TECHNICALITIES

The rest of this book is going to focus on the subtleties of technical analysis because it is the most common and the most intricate form of analysis used in trading. Technical analysis entails interpreting charts, as charts are visual and are the most popular analytical tool used by traders.

You have to be good or become good at recognizing patterns and trends. In other words, you will be closely analyzing time and price, together with other indicators of expected movement. Stock prices follow a pattern because they are controlled by the traders, people, and people are creatures of habit. Individuals operate based on memory and instinct, and, thus, repeat themselves, even mistakes.

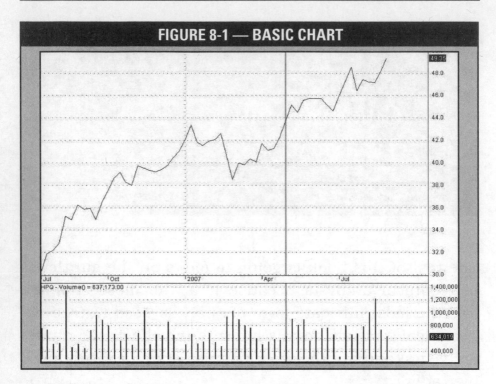

FIGURE 8-1 — BASIC CHART

All of this means that you have to become an expert at determining the habits of the collective mind of all of the traders trading in a specific stock. It all comes back to supply and demand, those two culprits talked about earlier. Look at the chart in Figure 8-1. As with all trading charts, it is a chart of price over time. You can see how the stock price can move up over time and how it can reverse and fall. It is like a mini map of the economy discussed in Chapter 7.

However, these charts can reveal so much more than a simple price change over time. You can also learn from it the volume of stocks being traded over time. The volume is recorded by the spikes in the lower part of the chart. When prices go up quickly over time, more traders are buying. The opposite is also true, of course. If stocks drop sharply, it is because lots of people are selling. Volume spikes on charts can show you exactly how many shares have been traded on any particular day, week, or year, depending on which type of chart you are using. Charts can also hold information on moving averages for the stocks, indicators, and oscillators that help traders "predict" what a stock might do next.

THE TRADING DAY

On trading day, you will not just see the business pattern on the charts. You will also see a pattern throughout the trading day. From the opening of the market to the closing of the market, there will be times during the day when certain things tend to happen. There is somewhat of a pattern to the trading day. However, having said this, you must know that the stock market performs in a predictable way, except when it does not. This means that you never know what will happen with the market from day to day, hour to hour, minute to minute, or second to second. This is precisely the challenge that makes trading fun, frustrating, and infuriating to the strictly logical mind and a touch of fortunetelling to the rest of us.

CHARTING BASICS

There are three types of price charts that traders should be familiar with: line charts, bar charts, and candlestick charts. They all give similar information in a slightly different fashion, and you may find that you like the readability of one type of chart over another. One thing to know about any chart is that it may give information for any number of designated periods. Charts may give trends that move over a week, a day, an hour, or five minutes. Thus, you should always be aware of what designated time period you are viewing when analyzing a chart so that you are interpreting the information correctly. Having said that, many forms or patterns repeat on a micro, mid- and macro time schedule, so you may see the same formation in a five-minute interval chart and in a one-month interval chart, for instance.

LINE CHARTS

Line charts are drawn by joining the points of the closing price for each of the designated time periods over time. For instance, in Figure 8-2, the line is drawn by joining the points that represent the closing prices for each day throughout the year.

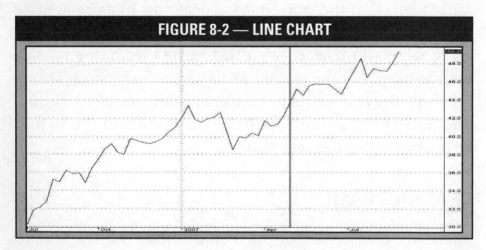

FIGURE 8-2 — LINE CHART

These charts help traders see the forest, the big picture, and when you overlay them, you can see when different trends move together and when they diverge. However, line charts do not offer themselves as the best analytical tool. Bar charts and candlestick charts give some additional information about the nature of the price movements, are easier to read and can disclose a tremendous amount of information in a small amount of space.

BAR CHARTS

Bar charts are a popular tool and are easy to read. Many traders rely on them. These charts are characterized by a vertical line that indicates the price range for the stock for that day (if it is a daily chart). The horizontal bar protruding from the left of the vertical bar represents the opening price for the day, and the horizontal bar protruding from the right represents the closing price for the day.

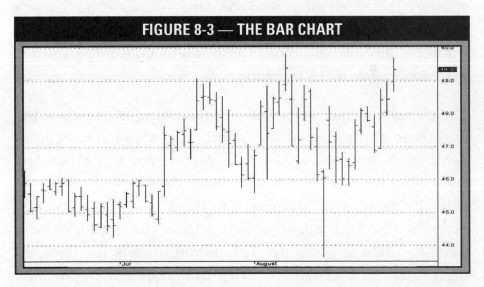

FIGURE 8-3 — THE BAR CHART

These charts are useful because, at a glance, you can see (on a daily chart) what the price range of the stock was over the day, at which price it opened, at which price it closed, and where these prices are in relation to one another. In other words, was the opening price higher or lower than the closing price? Was the lowest price of the day the opening or closing price? Was the highest price of the day the opening or closing price? Unlike the line chart, you can see how much the price varied in the day, which will give you an idea of volatile the dealing was. You can also have the same type of chart over longer periods, such as a week or a month.

It is worth thinking a little more deeply about what information you can get from the common bar chart, as this is a fundamental of the technical analysis. If the bar is long, it means that there was much variation in the price of deals during the day's trading, with buyers and sellers fighting over the price, and that would also mean much volume. The converse is also the case — a short bar means not much disagreement on price and maybe not much trading going on, although there might be a large volume with good agreement instead.

The horizontal tick to the left, representing the price of the first trade of the day, or the "open," can also tell us a great deal, but it may tell a false tale. More than any other, the open may be influenced by factors that have little to do with the underlying sentiment to the stock. If the opening price is up, you might assume that the traders think that the price is going up. This is not always the case, as there may be overnight activity that requires buying the stocks on opening, and the price may go back down to a more natural level an hour or two after the market starts. You might want to look at the daily charts to see if that particular stock is prone to this type of jump. It is common to have unusual effects at the market open, and you need to become familiar with them.

In contrast, the horizontal tick to the right, which represents the closing price, is accurate with the market sentiment, and may be the most important information on the bar. This is the value that is used when the whole range of day trading is not considered and only one number represents the day. If it is up above the previous day's close, it is called an up day, and that is a good indication that the buyers are enthusiastic and pushing a bull market.

THE CANDLESTICK CHART

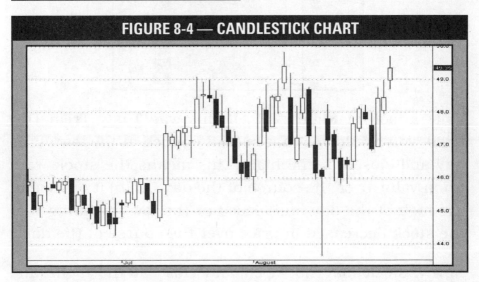

FIGURE 8-4 — CANDLESTICK CHART

Many people think that candlestick charts are the clearest price charts. They give you the information from a bar chart in a more visual format and are thus easier to read. They are in common use nowadays, so much so it is hard to believe that they were introduced to the West only in the early '90s by a trader named Steve Nison. Candlestick charts have been in use in Japan for many years, but Steve has said that candle charts are more than 1,000 years old. These charts are made using "real bodies" rather than just bars. These real bodies are colored either black or white. If one is white, the opening price was lower than the closing price, and if it is black, the opening price was higher than the closing price, i.e. the white body shows an increasing price, and the black body shows that the price fell over the day, or other period. The candlestick still shows the whole daily range, just like the bar, using a line which may extend above and below the real body.

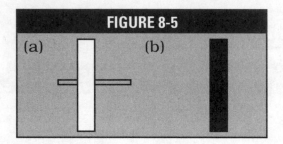

Take a look at Figure 8-5. If this was Tasty Treat Dog Food, you would see that in (a) it opened at the low of the day and closed at the high. This means the stock went up in value over the course of the day. In (b) it opened at the high of the day and closed at the low, meaning that the stock decreased in price over the course of the day.

Now a stock may not open and close at the highs and lows. It may reach a higher high during the day and then come back down or reach a lower low and come back up. This will look something like those in Figure 8-6. The lines above and below the real body show the limits of the prices reached during the day's trading, and these lines are called "shadows."

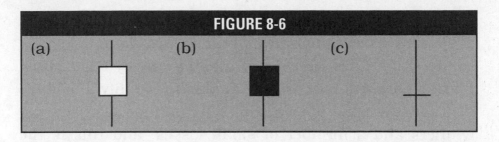

FIGURE 8-6

(a)   (b)   (c)

In (a), the price range went higher and lower during the day, yet the real body is white, so it still closed at a higher price than it opened with. In (b), the price range closed at a lower price than it opened with, and the daily trading again went above and below these values. In (c), there is no real body because, although the price ranged higher and lower than the opening and closing prices, in this case the stock opened and closed at the same price. There is a special name for this candlestick pattern — it is called a "doji," and it often means that the sentiment for the stock is neither bullish nor bearish, and traders are undecided about it. Often, it can be an indication that the direction of the price is about to change. Note that you can see exactly the same thing on a bar chart but that it is easier to see using a candlestick.

Candlestick bars normally need interpretation in relation to the pattern of candlesticks before and after them — one candlestick in isolation may be misleading.

INTERPRETING CANDLESTICK PATTERNS

Before you go into the other patterns you may look for in candlestick charts, it is best to state one important principle — there is no magic formula that will guarantee the same result each time. These patterns are indicators of trends or movements, and the reasoning behind each interpretation will be explained one by one. There will always be exceptions, and what we are doing is trying to stack the odds in favor of making money on trading. Some trades will lose; we are aiming to identify a balance of trades to come out on top. This may be by a few big winners and a number of small losses, and this is the pattern of many successful traders; or you may aim for lots of small winners and fewer losers. In virtually all trading, one of the keys is to quit a losing trade quickly, before it becomes a disaster, and this is so important I repeat it throughout the book.

In his Case Study, Stuart McPhee explains how he uses technical analysis, even to the exclusion of looking at the fundamentals. He also gives some good advice for potential traders.

SUCCESS STORY: STUART MCPHEE

Stuart McPhee is a private trader, author, and trading coach. He has written numerous articles and texts, including *Trading in a Nutshell, 2nd Edition*. He also conducts trading courses throughout Southeast Asia and has presented at trading expos in Singapore; Kuala Lumpur, Malaysia; Ho Chi Minh City, Vietnam; Shenzhen, China; and Bangkok, Thailand.

Visit Stuart's "Develop your Trading Plan" Web site, **www.trading-plan.com**, for detailed information on how to develop a trading plan that is right for you and that you will implement with confidence. Also available is a regular e-zine full of useful trading tips and ideas.

What types of trading are you involved with?	I trade two different markets and styles.
	For my conservative approach, which I trade through my superannuation (retirement) fund, I trade equities on the Australian Securities Exchange (ASX) from mainly the top 500 companies or All Ordinaries Index, and I do this on a risk-

SUCCESS STORY: STUART MCPHEE

	management basis. When you move outside the top 500, you expose yourself to the more volatile and speculative stocks, and they are the type that I am not that comfortable trading. By limiting yourself to the top 500, you are also generally ensuring that there is sufficient liquidity in the stocks and they move with some sense of stability. For a little more action, I trade Contracts for Difference (CFDs) on a limited number of top 50 stocks on the ASX. These two approaches result in vastly different styles in terms of many things, including time required, risk, and number of transactions. I personally use technicals and rarely consider the fundamentals before opening a position. This is not to say that I do not think fundamentals work or are effective — that is far from the case. I just do not use them, and I am not ashamed to admit that I have bought stock in companies previously and not known what those companies really did or whether or not they made money. I would have bought them because their price was heading higher and moving well — that was of most interest to me.
How did you start trading?	It was back in 1996 when my wife and I had some savings and wanted to do something with it. We did not consider property at that stage and almost automatically considered the stock market. We went to a broker to set up an account and in the early stages considered their advice to be golden. It would have been soon after that I thought how I could probably do the analysis myself and have more of an influence over what we were buying and selling.
What were your main concerns when starting trading?	To be honest, I probably did not have too many concerns when I first started. I thought it would be relatively easy. I was a very confident young man who was at that time a full-time Army officer, and I was used to starting new endeavors and succeeding. I recall first getting interested in the markets and thinking this was something I could take to with little effort. Soon after starting when a few trades did not work out for me, I started to be confused, as I could not appreciate why I was losing money. This

SUCCESS STORY: STUART MCPHEE

	was a humbling experience for me but a very positive one. It was from this point onwards, that it became obvious I needed some further guidance and education.
How soon did you see a steady flow of income?	It was throughout 1999 when I started to make better trading decisions and see some benefit from trading. The profits became faster and thicker as that year came to a close and the NASDAQ began to surge higher.
What are your likes and dislikes about trading?	The biggest likes would have to be the fact that you can really do it from anywhere, and technological advances are making this easier every day. I think the other major like for trading is being self-employed — being your own boss. A lot of people dream of this idea, whether it be in trading the markets or other. The overheads (expenses) are minimal, and it does not require a huge amount of capital to start. Probably the best thing I like is the flexibility with your time. Time is becoming so precious for so many people now, and with trading, you can easily choose when you trade and when you do not.
	The dislikes can be quite numerous too. At times, it can become stressful and emotional, and when you are risking your own money, this is almost inevitable. I am happy to say that this has decreased over the years. The other significant dislike is the solitary nature of it. My background is from a military organization where teamwork and camaraderie underpin the culture, and there are times now when I miss working with other people as part of a dynamic organization.
What personal qualities helped you to become a trader?	Disciplined and organized would be the two main ones. I will be the first to admit that my time in the military starting way back at the Royal Military College, Duntroon, (Australia) undergoing intensive officer training has provided me some great skills and attributes to trade well — none more important than discipline.
	Discipline has helped me greatly with my trading as well as other areas in my life. It is discipline that makes me feel comfortable with deciding on what has to be done in accordance with my trading plan, as opposed to what I really want to do or would feel the most comfortable doing.
	The other would be organization skills. I hate being ill prepared

	SUCCESS STORY: STUART MCPHEE
	with anything, and this has certainly helped in my trading. I am a planner who always likes to be prepared to undertake something.
What is the biggest challenge you have faced in trading?	The biggest challenge would have been accepting losses earlier on. Like everyone, when I first started, I did not like having losing trades. I think it was probably reading the *Market Wizards* book by Jack Schwager (which I still say has had the most influence of anything on my trading life) that made me realize that even the very successful traders all had losing trades. Not every trade was profitable. So, I realized in that sense, I was not any different to them. The difference was how they reacted to those losing trades. All of the traders interviewed in that book (without exception) emphasized that cutting losses was one of the most important things (if not the most important) they did! The fact that they all said it, despite their vast array of different trading approaches, meant a lot to me and convinced me of the importance of doing it. This was a turning point in my trading.
What advice would you give potential traders?	It depends. If you are certain that the recipient of the advice is willing to accept what you say and run with it, I would tell them about the importance of the right mind-set (or psychology) for trading and talk about how to prepare themselves for the mental rigors of trading. The problem here is that if you tell someone who is starting to trade that their mind-set or psychology is going to be the most important part of their success (and not their entry signal, for example), most would just laugh at you and think you are joking. Here is the irony of trading — the primary reason why people trade is to make money. Yet, it is the money that often causes people to make all the mistakes and not make money, because they focus too much on it. For example, the most important thing you can do when trading is to cut your losses, yet deep down people do not want to

SUCCESS STORY: STUART MCPHEE

because it appears to go against the primary reason why you are trading — to make money. By cutting the loss, you are denying yourself the opportunity to make back the money in that trade.

The other thing with money is that I do not think there are many other things in life that affect our emotions as much as money does. So when we are trading and our own money is on the line, it is difficult to not get too emotional with our decisions, yet emotions often lead us to making poor trading decisions.

Trading is decision making. Often, you are faced with several alternatives of what you can decide to do; however, generally it boils down to two options. You either decide with what you feel like doing, or you decide with what you know has to be done to trade well. Most people select the former, whereas those who are successful with their trading, ignore what they feel like doing and do what has to be done to ensure overall long-term success. This is a key separator between successful traders and the rest.

Aside from the psychology response, I would tell a beginner that trading is not as easy as you probably think it is. Many people think that trading is easy money, as I did early on — it is probably the hardest easy money there is.

If a new trader can appreciate right from the start that trading is not as easy as they think it is, they will most likely approach it with a more committed effort and be prepared for the challenges that trading presents.

With the benefit of experience, there are so many things I wish I knew when I first started that I now just accept and take as "the way it is." I could have also answered with:

- Be humble — you are not going to get every trade right.

- Be committed — trading is not easy, and any half-hearted attempts will not get you anywhere.

- Educate yourself — there is so much to learn and while you can learn from actually trading, you can save yourself a lot of money and stress by learning from someone else who has come before you.

SUCCESS STORY: STUART MCPHEE

	• Take it slowly/be patient — trading success is not going to happen overnight. For most people, this is a lifelong endeavor, so does it really matter if it takes you a few years to start trading profitably? • Keep it simple — people have a tendency to overcomplicate matters and develop intricate and complex solutions to problems. When we accept that trading is not easy, we think only a complex solution (trading plan) will work. In trading, simple does work. It also makes it much easier for us to follow the plan when it is simple. • Be realistic — having high expectations of yourself is a good thing; however, unrealistic expectations is not. Many traders, when presented with the wonderful opportunities that the market offers, can be very easily led to setting unrealistic goals for their trading. This can be devastating. It is vital to set goals with your trading, but it is equally vital to ensure that those goals are measurable and realistic. • Focus on the right things — do not focus too much on your entry signal, as most people do. Keep it simple, and then move onto the more important areas like position-sizing, setting exits, and preparing your mind for successful, disciplined trading. • Whatever you do, protect your capital — it goes without saying that if you have no money left, you cannot make money. This is an important issue because any new trader is not focused on protecting their money; they are focused solely on making money.
What qualities do you think are important in a would-be trader?	There are many qualities or character attributes that successful traders have. I will go through and name a few. Let us start with perseverance. As Calvin Coolidge, the 30th president of the United States said in one of my favorite quotes, "The slogan 'Press On' has solved and always will solve the problems of the human race." Other similar terms include commitment and determination. For traders, this provides us the ability to continue on in the toughest of times even when

SUCCESS STORY: STUART MCPHEE

everything appears all too much. It is the edge that allows us to climb the walls that are obstacles when everyone else around us turns away from the wall and does something else.

Another important attribute is humility. All traders enter trades that lose money — you cannot simply get every trade right. You will find the very best traders are very humble, and they are the best losers. Successful traders never move stops and accept losing as part and parcel of trading. They are also not afraid to learn from others and admit they do not know everything.

Another one is patience. You are not provided with great trading opportunities every day, and the best traders are patient enough to wait long enough for high probability trades to come their way. Financial markets are here to stay — they underpin the corporate arena in every country around the world, so they are not going anywhere. Trading success is not going to happen overnight. For most people, this is a lifelong endeavor, so does it really matter if it takes you a few years to start trading profitably?

How about responsibility? Successful traders make their own trading decisions based on their own analysis and trading plan, but more importantly do not blame anyone or anything else when it does not work out and they lose money in a trade. In a world nowadays where there is a clear trend of people looking for someone else to blame for their own actions, this is probably becoming less obvious. The key is to be an adult and take responsibility for your own actions — you are solely responsible for your own success and failures.

Successful traders are also conservative and very defensive. Even though their primary motivation is to make money (as it is for all of us), they adopt a very defensive mind-set and focus not so much on making money, but more so on protecting the money they have. This means they set and stick to stops and risk very little of their account on any individual trade.

With anything in life, confidence is important — trading is no exception. Confidence in yourself and the trading plan you develop. One thing that will help with your confidence is your own knowledge and understanding of the markets, the products

SUCCESS STORY: STUART MCPHEE

you are trading, and various tools you use in your decision making. Most importantly however, competence yields confidence. If you are not competent at something, it is highly unlikely that you will be confident doing it.

There are many other attributes that could also be listed here, to include emotional control and stability, organizational skills, and honesty. There is no doubt that all of these are correct and valuable to possess; however, I think there is none more important than discipline.

Discipline is the level of self-control you have. Trading all boils down to decision making, and often the decisions that need to be made are difficult. Let us consider the options we have. For any individual decision, there are often two options available to us. The first option is the decision that will make us feel most comfortable and the one that we really want to take. The second option is the one that follows our trading plan. Most often these will be two very different outcomes.

There is one thing that assists us to take the second option and not the first — discipline. I believe a key separator between successful traders and the rest is they will act first upon their trading plan and not what they feel like doing. Most traders make the decision that makes them feel the most comfortable, whether this is letting a loss continue or to cut a profit short in order to realize some money.

When they feel super-confident about a trade, successful traders do not allow greed to consume them and commit more money into the trade. They trade according to their trading plan — they adhere to the money management rules in their trading plan.

Here is what happens … we have our mind set on long-term successful trading; however, other things influence our actions/ trading decisions, like emotions, our short-term needs, and our present mood. These tend to overpower any long-term goals we have, so we will often pursue short-term pleasures and by doing so, avoid short-term discomfort, at the expense of our longer-term goals and rewards. It is human nature.

SUCCESS STORY: STUART MCPHEE

When did you know that you would be successful?	Great question! Reading *Market Wizards* by Jack Schwager was probably the one thing that ultimately had the greatest influence on my trading. It was from reading this book and gaining an insight into the minds of some highly successful traders that I realized some vital ingredients to trading well. These were things like cutting losses, managing risk, and following a plan. I knew I had the discipline and organizational skills to make this work, so it was this book in combination with some significant losses that made me realize I was going to be a successful trader.
What is the biggest trading mistake you ever made?	In late 1999 and early 2000, I was trading very actively, as many people were at the time, as the NASDAQ was climbing very strongly and this flowed onto numerous technology companies in Australia. Once this all came crashing down a few months later, I suffered some significant losses. Those losses really hurt me emotionally and financially. When I took time to reflect on that time, I realized that if I wanted to make this trading thing work for me, I had to cut losses whether I liked it or not. I remember committing to myself that from then on I was going to do everything in my power to cut losses when a trade did not head in the direction I had anticipated. So the combination of some painful losses myself and reading *Market Wizards* has led me to not have one issue with taking a loss in a trade. I appreciate that it is one of the most important things I can do — there is almost a sense of relief when I do exit a losing trade because I have totally eliminated the possibility of any further loss. This is a good thing, because most traders know that if you do not cut a loss when you should, it only gets more difficult to do if the loss grows. As the loss gets bigger, it just gets harder and harder. The easiest it will ever be to cut is right at the beginning when it is only very small.
Which stock indicator do you pay the most attention to?	Earlier on, I went through the search looking for the right indicator to use, and every time I heard someone else present a seminar about trading, I ended up considering the indicators that the presenter had on his charts during the presentation. I used to think like a lot of people do, and that is, "If he is using them, then they must work, so I am going to use them."

	SUCCESS STORY: STUART MCPHEE
	There are many popular indicators that are widely used, like the MACD, Stochastic Oscillator, Relative Strength Index, Directional Movement, and the list goes on. However, I do not use any of them, and have not for a number of years now.
	I am not saying that the indicators above do not work or they will not assist you with your trading. I have challenged the various indicators to see if they would provide me a significant advantage in my trading, and for me, they all came up with a negative response. I therefore questioned the need to use any of them in my trading. The truth is that no indicator is infallible, and they will often provide a false signal. If they do not provide a marked advantage to you, if they do not provide you an edge, then why use them?
	The only indicators I use are a moving average and a couple of very simple indicators I developed myself, and their use is limited to my entry decision. The whole premise behind my use of indicators is to keep it simple.
Describe your setup of computer, software, and Internet connection.	There is nothing elaborate in my trading setup. I use a laptop, for its obvious advantages, with a cable Internet connection. I have used MetaStock since 1999 and find it very useful. I obtain live data through my broker's Web site.

In the previous section I introduced the doji pattern, where the real body of the candlestick is just a line, which comes from the opening and closing prices being the same. I said that this showed indecision on the part of the market, with neither the bulls nor the bears deciding on the direction that the price should go and which may mean a change in direction of the price. If it comes in a rising trend and follows a long white bar, this is particularly a sign that the market's enthusiasm for the stock is becoming tired and a reversal may be coming. An even clearer indication of this is when there is no lower shadow — the opening price, lowest price, and closing price were all the same, with some prices higher during the day. The higher prices did not stick, which again shows the bears winning at the end of the day and an expected downturn.

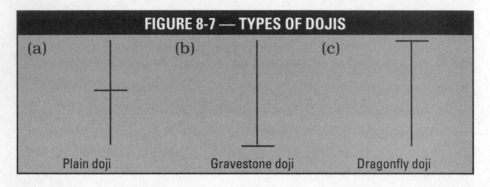

FIGURE 8-7 — TYPES OF DOJIS

(a) Plain doji   (b) Gravestone doji   (c) Dragonfly doji

On the other hand, if you see the same doji with no lower shadow (Fig. 8-7 [b]) after a downtrend in price, it could indicate some strength appearing in buying the stock. Even though it is not enough to stick until the close, it may signal an interest starting that will result in the price rising. This is a gravestone doji.

The opposite type of doji, with no upper shadow, is called a dragonfly doji (Fig. 8-7 [c]) and also gives a clear indication of a change in a trend. No upper shadow shows that the opening price, highest price, and the closing price were the same, and there were some deals during the day at a lower price. If this comes after a period of increasing prices, the bulls did not succeed in establishing a higher price, and the bears managed to push the price down during the day, so, although the lower prices did not stick, this doji may indicate the end of the uptrend. If it comes after a downtrend, it shows that the bear movement did not last until the close and may signal that the lowest price has been reached.

A more general example of the doji idea is given by the spinning top pattern. Named after the children's toy, these are black or white candlesticks where the real body is short. They show that the market may be running out of steam for the current direction of movement and can give an early warning that the trend is coming to an end.

Another candlestick pattern that is a good indicator is called the hammer. This has a long lower shadow and little or no upper shadow. It looks like a hammer, and you can think of it as hammering out the base price. It shows that the market has tested a lower price and rejected it by the time of the close. Technically, it is said that the hammer should have a lower shadow that is at least twice the length of the body — the body can be black or white. The market may go up shortly, although if a subsequent day closes under the hammer's low, the opposite may be true.

Finally, you should look at what is called an engulfing pattern. This is formed from two candlesticks and is a small real body followed by a larger real body of the opposite color, both higher at the top than the small body and lower at the bottom — engulfing the earlier values. A bullish engulfing pattern has a small black body followed by a large white body on the next day, or trading period. This will signal the reversing of the downward trend. It is easy to see why. The white body starts below the black body; that is, the opening price on the second day is below the previous close. However, the price rises steeply to pass the previous open, which is a strong indication of the bullish tendency, which we may reasonably expect to continue. The black body being short is also reminiscent of the doji, indicating the likelihood of a reversal and showing a near balance between supply and demand.

A bearish engulfing pattern is the opposite. A small white body is engulfed on the next day by a black bearish body, which tends to show that the bears are taking control of the price and will drive it down.

If you do not have an account yet, as an exercise go to the Yahoo! or MSN finance section, look up any stock, and click through to the candlestick chart. See how many of the above features you can spot. You should note that the indicators do not work all the time, but you should be able to see the truth in the above analyses. It can help to print out a few charts and annotate them for reference. By the way, well done! You have just started thinking for yourself about trading and developing your own understanding, which will lead to the emergence of your own personalized trading system.

In summary, the candlestick chart is a visual way to see what the market is doing and a powerful tool in your armory for determining how and where to trade. You can get more detailed information from **www.candlecharts.com**, which is Steve Nison's Web site. Although some traders rely on candles for their technical analysis, we are going to look at many more aspects that can be considered so that we finish with an understanding of the full spectrum of trading tools.

SUCCESS BULLETS

- The basic starting point is the chart of price change

over time, which can also have volume and other indicators.

- Large price movements tend to be associated with a large volume of trading.

- Line charts show the closing prices over time and give a picture of the stock.

- Bar charts give additional information, including the range of prices during the day.

- Many traders think that candlestick charts are the clearest to read. They show the opening price, the closing price, and the range of prices during the day.

- The white body means that the closing price was above the opening price.

- The black body denotes that the close was below the open, that the price dropped.

- All candlestick forms should be considered in relation to the shapes before.

- The doji form, which has a real body length of zero, that is, the opening price equaled the closing price, is a sign of change.

- The engulfing pattern, where the next day's candlestick has an opposite color, and the bottom lower and the top higher than the previous, is a good sign of a change in sentiment.

WORDS TO KNOW

Bar chart, candlestick chart, doji, dragonfly doji, engulfing pattern, gravestone doji, hammer, line chart, oscillators, spinning top

Support & Resistance — Is This a Revolution?

Now it is time to take charting one step further. Traders talk of "support" and "resistance," the common meanings of which are obvious, but as a trader you need to quantify these and take them one step further than generalities.

Again we start with a chart of stock prices over time. In this case, we do not mind if it is a bar or a candlestick chart — they graph the same data — as we are looking at the highs and/or the lows of each day's trading. We need to start by understanding trend lines — these are straight lines that would be drawn on the trading chart or may be added by using charting software — that show the movement, or trend, of the stock price.

The first point to note about trend lines is that there is no one right answer, or trend line. As the market continues, you may have to rethink your trend line several times, even if you think that you have a good representation of the price movement when you first draw it.

The market is dynamic, and trends do not last forever. Intimately bound up in this whole concept is also your "horizon" as a trader; you will see the chart and the trend differently if you are an intraday trader, an end-of-day trader, or if you review only your stocks at the end of each week.

Following on from this point, you should appreciate that sometimes it is not possible to draw a trend line that means anything. Stocks may meander in price, with no one direction being dominant, and any trend line you draw in such a case becomes pointless and arbitrary.

You can try changing the time scale of the chart to see if a trend appears, but be prepared to be confounded at times. Do not be afraid to try several lines to see which one appeals to you as the "best fit."

With all that said, look at Figure 9-1. This illustrates a stock that has an uptrend, with a small downtrend in the middle of the rise.

See how you can draw a trend line from the low to the high price, and you can draw three trend lines, one for the first rise in price, one for the downtrend, then one for the final rise. Which is correct, the single line or the three lines?

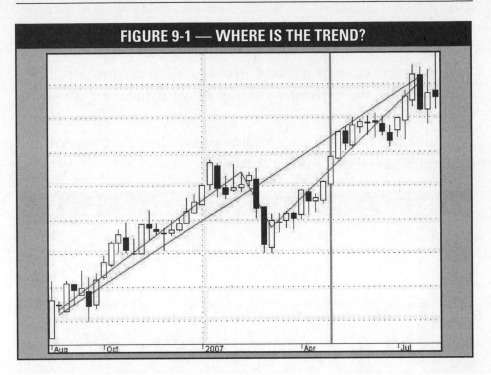

FIGURE 9-1 — WHERE IS THE TREND?

If you have been paying attention, you would know that was a trick question. The answer is both, or neither, or either one. It depends what you need from the chart and what your schedule for trading is. You should notice that trend lines may show you what you want, and you should work hard to try and keep them objective if they are to have any value to you.

Note that, unlike candlestick charts, a trend line does not have much to say about the best points to enter or exit a trade. The trend line is perfect with hindsight, but nothing in particular happens to a trend line to signify that the stock has hit its lowest low, or its highest high. You have to look a little bit deeper at the information available to you to get more clues to help with this.

SUPPORT LINE

A particular case of a trend line is called a "support line." This can be thought of as supporting a price at a certain level and not permitting it to drop below. Of course, this is not literally true, as exceptions prove, but it is a common pattern that is quite often followed.

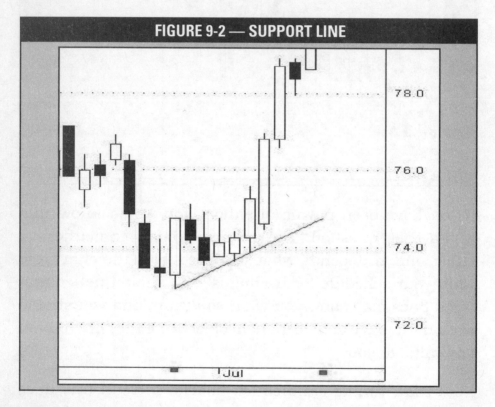

FIGURE 9-2 — SUPPORT LINE

Look at Figure 9-2, where the stock price is rising. There is an uptrend. You may also notice that this follows a bullish engulfing pattern. The support line is drawn by joining the lowest low to the next low on the uptrend. You then have a line, which is rising in price over time, which can be extended upward as time passes.

The support line can be used for timing entry and exit from

the stock as follows. Continue tracking the stock price and extending the support line. If and when the stock hits a new higher low price, which comes down to and touches the support line, then goes back up, this signals that the support line is valid and gives a point at which you may want to buy the stock. You can see that after the third touch in Figure 9-2 the price rose higher (note that Figure 9-2 is not as complex as most charts you will consider but is selected to demonstrate the principle clearly). The price of the stock is rising, and the higher lows affirm that buyers feel the value is increasing. If the stock keeps coming down to touch the support line and does not drop through it, then these additional points are considered to be tests of the support, which provide more evidence that the increasing price is supported by the market.

When a time is reached that the stock price drops below the support line, you should consider selling, or exiting, the stock, as this indicates that the support is broken and cannot be relied upon anymore. Any time the price goes through a line that was being followed, it is called a breakout and means that the line cannot be trusted any more. A breakout often means that a trend is coming to an end.

In contrast to the support line being tested and surviving, as outlined above, there are some traders who will draw a support line on the basis of two lows and enter the market without waiting for a third. I regard this as more "seat of the pants" trading, as there are many ways to interpret the formation of the line. Such a way does exist, and you should try and avoid it until you are experienced enough to be comfortable with it.

You should be able to see that this is not an exact science. The lines could be drawn in a different and seemingly equally valid way. The breakout may not be large or obvious. Even with all the factors falling into place, the stock could still behave differently from the historical expectation. However, we are trying to play the odds here, making enough moves that we get a selection of winning trades and make more profit from the winners than loss from the losers. The support line is another tool that you can use to consider how and where to trade.

RESISTANCE LINE

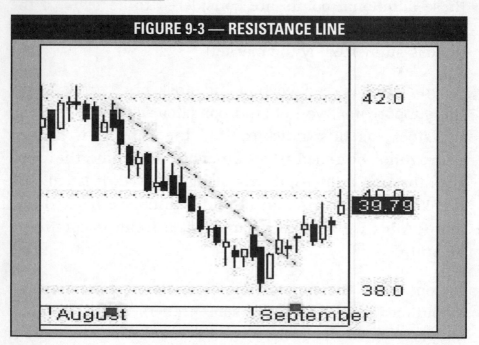

FIGURE 9-3 — RESISTANCE LINE

The resistance line is similar to the support line, but it approaches from the other side. Resistance is drawn by connecting highs rather than lows, where the price backs off each time, showing resistance by the buyers to paying a higher price, and is on a downward trend. As a trader interpreting the signs, you might expect sellers to take a profit here, as it is as high as they think the market will go before sinking some more. If you do not already own the stock — and, if you did, we hope you got out before the downward trend — you may think the resistance line does not matter much to you, but it can be used similarly to the support line. You can take it that this is the limit line for the market, so if you have a breakout — in this case to the upside — this may signify a change of trend and show you a possible time to get into the stock, as illustrated above. Just as with the support line, when the graph touches but does not cross the line, this is called a test of resistance and tends to reinforce your confidence that the line is correct, at least for the time being.

By their nature, all these trends are dynamic, and that means that lines often do not last long before being violated and needing to be redrawn. However, trend lines can tell you a lot about the market's attitude to a stock's price, and as such are crucial to the success of your trading efforts. You need to know how, when, and why to draw trend lines and how to interpret them to truly succeed.

CHANNELS

While you are looking at simple straight lines that try to track the stock price movements, you should consider simple channels. In their fundamental terms, channels are just a support and a resistance line enclosing the stock price, although the two lines are drawn parallel, so some juggling is needed. You will draw the channel by starting either with a support line, joining at least two lowest low points, and drawing a top line parallel touching the highest point, or vice versa, starting with a resistance line touching a minimum of two points and drawing a lower line. If and when you get the price testing the line — touching and not breaking it — then you can be more confident that you have a good channel.

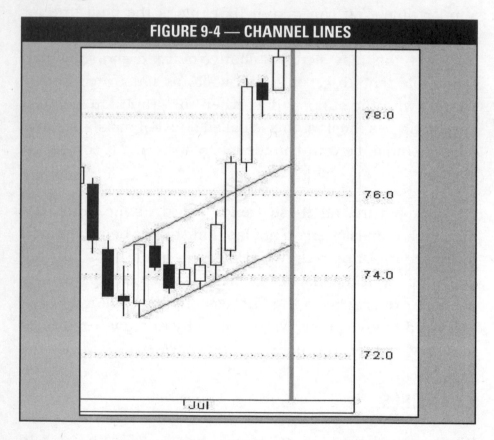

FIGURE 9-4 — CHANNEL LINES

You can see the principle of the channel — two lines within which the price is expected to vary, but if it crosses either of the channel lines, you have a breakout and can anticipate changes. The channel provides a visual track that allows you to more clearly see what movements are within the norm and when something else appears to be happening.

You can use the channel in various ways — while the channel lasts, you can buy at the lower point and sell at the top, repeatedly. You can also set yourself a stop-loss at the lower line, so that if the price breaks out downward, you are selling the stock as rapidly as possible.

The danger here is the same as with single support and resistance lines — is a breakout real, or is it just a minor glitch and the price will return to the channel? This is not a perfect world, and the markets are far from reacting as we would expect. Jump on an upward breakout too soon, and you risk the price dropping back to the channel; jump off too soon with a downward trend, and you may have settled for less than you need have. As you realize by now, there is no way that we can answer that without 20/20 hindsight. You can, however, gauge the move against other indicators and try to form a consensus solution on the reality of the move. You will develop your own style of trading and learn which figures you prefer to rely on.

As with all the previous lines, you may have to redraw the channel lines often to get what seems to be a best fit, and they are subjective in that respect. They are just another visual assistance and should be read in conjunction with other tools, which may confirm or deny your ideas.

FIBONACCI RETRACEMENTS

Leonardo of Pisa, also known by other names, including the now famous Fibonacci, was an Italian mathematician who lived in the 12th and 13th centuries. He receives credit for a sequence of numbers that he used in his *Book of Calculation*. He did not discover the sequence — it was known about in India in the 6th century — but he used it to demonstrate the reproduction rate of rabbits in a problem in his book, and this may have been its introduction to the West.

The sequence is easily calculated, each term being the sum of the two previous numbers, after starting with an initial 0 and 1. Thus the first terms are 0, 1, 1, 2, 3, 5, 8, 13, 21, 34, 55, and 89. As the sequence progresses, the ratio between two adjacent numbers comes closer to the "golden ratio," as it was called by the Greeks, which is 1.618054, or, taken the other way around, 0.618054. The ratio is the inverse of the ratio less one, which provides an easy way to calculate it (for mathematicians).

The point of the foregoing is that many things in nature reflect these ratios — the branching of trees, florets of a pineapple, and seeds in a sunflower head, for example. It is the ratio that is most pleasing to the eye, used in architecture through the ages and even in playing cards. About trading, the theory is that lines drawn at the intervals relating to the Fibonacci numbers somehow mark the turning points, or retracements, of the stock price move and define the support and resistance levels.

Your software will have the availability to draw these lines automatically on the price charts. If you experiment with different starting and ending points for the trend line associated with the Fibonacci lines, you may find some correlation to the turning points. Some traders think these "Fibs" are predictive indicators, and this may be self-fulfilling — traders use them as indicators for making moves, so the market is influenced at these values. As all indicators work sometimes and not at other times, it is difficult to prove their real value, but they are there if you want to try them out.

SUCCESS BULLETS

- Trend lines can be drawn on a price chart and give an indication of the stock's movement.

- Trend lines are dynamic and may need revision to find the best fit.

- The support line represents support for the price, that is, the lowest line that we expect the price to drop to. It can be drawn on the basis of two low points, but three points give more validity to the location of the support.

- The resistance line is similar to the support line but represents the top limit of the price, where there is resistance to any higher price.

- A breakout occurs when a support or resistance line is clearly passed and the price goes outside the range indicated.

- A breakout often indicates a change in the trend and can be a signal for trading.

- A channel is two lines drawn parallel either side of the stock price and represents the limits between which you expect the price to oscillate. This can be traded repeatedly from the lower support line to the higher.

- Fibonacci lines can indicate retracement, or turning point, levels.

WORDS TO KNOW

Breakout, channel, Fibonacci, resistance, retracement, support

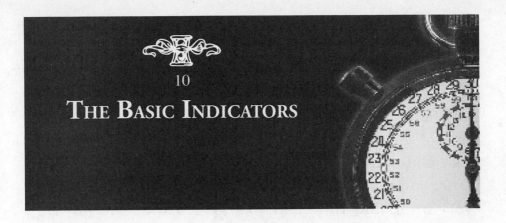

10

THE BASIC INDICATORS

You may wonder, at this stage, if you have explored most of the factors to do with finding a stock to trade; after all, you have covered not just the closing prices, as reported in the newspapers each day, but also the opening and the maximum and minimum prices reached during the day, and you have drawn lines to track the stock's progress. The fact that you are only just over halfway through this book may, however, give you the suspicion that there is still much ground to cover, and you would be correct.

PATTERNS

You will notice after looking at a few charts that the price movements form patterns that repeat across different times and different stocks. Members of a branch of the trading fraternity have trained to recognize many patterns and use them as the basis for considering a trade, subsequently viewing the numbers or indicators for verification. This is distinct from the other approach, which requires calculations, inevitably nowadays done relatively painlessly on a computer, to sift through potential stock prospects. There is something to be said for both approaches, although the pattern method requires experience and may never be mastered, at least to the point of profiting, so I would recommend that you use the statistical method to identify your trades at the start of your career. If you are interested in educating yourself further, as you need to be to keep on top of your game, you may want to observe the patterns leading into every trade that you make to start learning the ways.

That said, a review of the common patterns that you might see will help you in understanding what you are looking at and give some knowledge of the basic reasons for the movements. You can expect stock prices moving even in a trend to have periods of consolidation, so you get a pattern similar to sawteeth, lunging forward, and then taking a breath as it were, before the next lunge.

When the stocks are not trending, they will range up and down at the same level. You should watch out for prices that vary chaotically and do not have a good pattern, as these are hard to anticipate and trade reliably. These results are referred to as congestion patterns for obvious reasons.

The Case Study from Sean Hyman speaks to the validity of pattern following — after trend lines give a first-level analysis, he looks for favorable patterns, as he explains.

SUCCESS STORY: SEAN HYMAN

Sean Hyman — Currency Director, Editor of *The Money-Trader*

Sean has close to 15 years experience as a stockbroker, manager, and trader. He became interested in the financial markets at a young age and decided to work for Charles Schwab in Orlando, Florida. He later went on to run a technical analysis "call in" line for their million dollar-plus clients and active traders.

After that, he went on to work at Forex Capital Markets (FXCM) as an FX Power Course Instructor. There he taught online traders around the world each day how to trade currencies. In addition to this he wrote market commentaries for FXCM, DailyFX, and **istockanalyst.com**. Through the years, he has refined his trading approach through the use of fundamental/technical analysis and intermarket analysis. In addition to his role as *Money Trader* editor, Sean also acts as currency director for the Sovereign Society. He is a regular contributor to *The Offshore A-Letter*, *My Two Cents*, and *The Sovereign Individual*, a monthly global investment and asset protection newsletter, as well as speaking at conferences and expos on the behalf of Sovereign Society both nationally and internationally.

What types of trading are you involved with?	I trade the currency market or what some refer to as the spot Forex market. I look at daily, one-year charts … four-hour, 40-day charts and one-hour, 30-day charts.
How did you start trading?	I actually got my start in stocks. I traded them for a number of years before I found my way to Forex. I love the 24-hour-a-day trading aspect of currencies as well as the lack of commissions. (In Forex trading, you pay only the spread.)
What were your main concerns when starting trading?	Would I be able to become successful at it, and where in the world do I start? (Ha ha.)
How soon did you see a steady flow of income?	When I started in stocks, I did very well. For instance my first project was helping a relative of mine grow their 401K. We mushroomed it from $40,000 to over $330,000 dollars in about five to six years' time with no leverage of course. Needless to say, I'm their favorite relative. (Ha ha.)
What are your likes and dislikes about trading?	I love the challenge of the game. I love it that patience is a requirement. This is what most people dislike about trading.

SUCCESS STORY: SEAN HYMAN

What personal qualities helped you to become a trader?	I'm a Christian ... so I think a solid moral character helps one to trade. After all, you are taught self control/patience, forgiveness, etc. All of these attributes calm the emotions and produce maturity in our thought processes. So things like this I believe help a trader a lot. After all, trading really tells you more about yourself than most things out there.
What is the biggest challenge you have faced in trading?	Finding good sources to learn from: mentors, good books, etc. There is a lot of junk out there.
What advice would you give potential traders?	Get an education in the market you are going to trade before jumping in alone, or have a mentor to come along beside you and help you in the early years of trading.
What qualities do you think are important in a would-be trader?	Discipline, patience, an even temper, consistency.
When did you know that you would be successful?	When I knew that I wanted it more than many out there. Passion is what should drive a person. If you are not passionate, then you are not going to be on top.
Describe your typical day.	I start off by reading the news overnight and looking at the daily charts of all the currency pairs that I watch. I look to see if there is something out there that gives one of them a leg up on the rest, or if there is an easy way to pick on one with bad news. After all, you need an edge coupled with good risk management in order to be successful.
What is the biggest trading mistake you ever made?	Taking a countertrend trade (trading against the main trend). Sometimes you can think something should turn down, and fundamentally it should. However, markets can hold to extremes much longer than they practically should. That is the nature of the beast.

SUCCESS STORY: SEAN HYMAN	
Which stock indicator do you pay the most attention to?	I use trend lines and support/resistance lines as my "tier 1" indicators. However, charting patterns (head and shoulders, triangles, etc.) are another thing that I look for. Afterward I may use a moving average or the MACD (moving average convergence divergence) indicator.

CONTINUATION PATTERNS

First consider what are called continuation patterns. The other main type of pattern is the reversal pattern, discussed later. Continuation patterns are places of consolidation in the stock's price and presage a breakout up or down. The stock may continue with its current trend after consolidation, but not always.

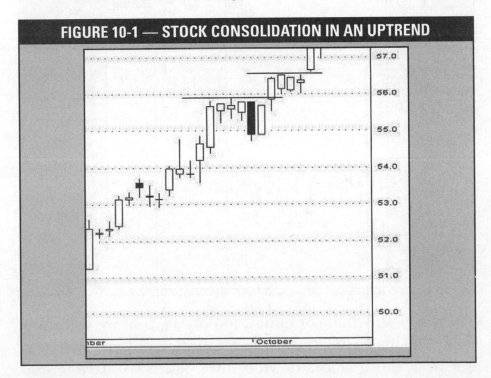

FIGURE 10-1 — STOCK CONSOLIDATION IN AN UPTREND

When the price consolidates, it will remain fairly stable, and the price will proceed horizontally (Figure 10-1). This example shows two consolidations in an underlying uptrend, and this is called a line continuation.

The next continuation pattern to be considered is the triangle, which can also be called the pennant. The price range reduces over time to form the triangle shape (Figure 10-2). This is a stronger indication for the trader, as the reduction in price range brings matters to a head in a reasonable time. If you watch it for a breakout, then you should get in on the move quickly.

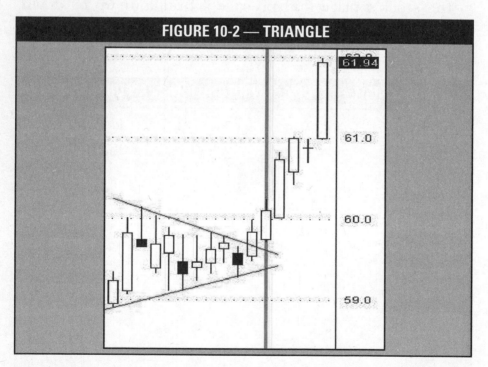

FIGURE 10-2 — TRIANGLE

The flag is the final continuation pattern that we will show here. The flag is like the line continuation pattern shown in Fig. 10-1, but it slopes down or up (Figure 10-3). Note that this example shows a slope down in an uptrend, which is a common configuration, and represents a price pullback before getting up steam to increase again.

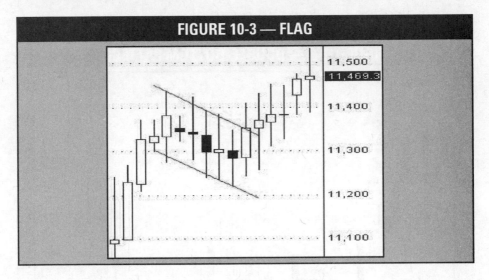

FIGURE 10-3 — FLAG

REVERSAL PATTERNS

Again, there are many reversal patterns, and you may learn to recognize them after some time and additional study. Some basic common patterns will be shown so that you have a starting point to explore this side of charting.

The first to consider is the double-bottom pattern (Figure 10-4). The reason for the name is obvious, but what is not so obvious is that this is quite a powerful indication of the stock's value and prospects. As you have seen in the previous chapter, the movement down then bouncing up twice is called a test of the support and gives an indication that the stock is ready to rise. If the price goes down and bounces up a third time, it is even more a proof that the value is holding, and some say that it indicates a higher move when and if it breaks out upward. A slightly different variation on this is called the reverse head-and-shoulders, where the middle low is below the adjacent lows, and this too is considered a good indication of a low and reversal.

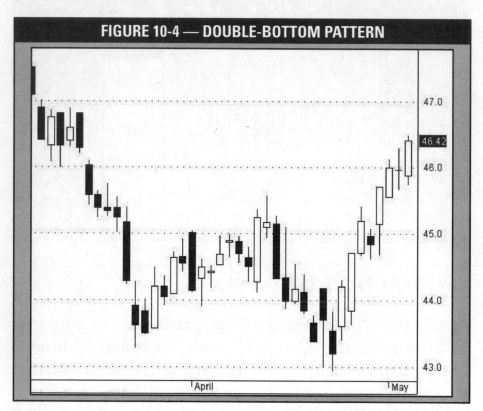

FIGURE 10-4 — DOUBLE-BOTTOM PATTERN

The other pattern is due to William O'Neil of *Investor's Business Daily*, and is called a cup-with-handle pattern (Figure 10-5). You can expect a period of consolidation after the handle section, and the longer the consolidation, the better the breakout.

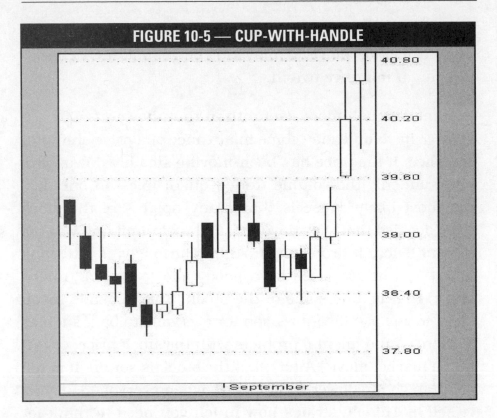

FIGURE 10-5 — CUP-WITH-HANDLE

VOLUME

The major item of information about a stock trading that we touched only on briefly in Chapter 8 is the volume traded. The volume is the number of stocks traded in a period, for our purposes most often in a day. Volume is a strong indicator to which you need to pay close attention. In addition to providing its own indication of price moves, it can confirm or deny the likelihood of a price move suggested by other indicators.

For a general move of the price up or down, if there is an increase in volume, it suggests that the move is anticipated and wanted by other traders in the market.

The opposite of course applies — if there is little volume behind a price move, it may not be a sustained change but just a minority twitch.

Volume is much more useful than that, however. Often, a change in volume may come in advance of a price shift. For instance, if the price has been moving steadily downward, and suddenly the volume traded quadruples on one day, the most likely cause is that many holders of the stock have decided that they have reached their limit and want to get out before it drops any further. Curiously, if you think about it, this may well be a good time to go long in the stock, that is, buy some of the stock. This depends if you can see any significant reason for everyone to bail, such as is there a fundamental problem with the stock price, or is it just a market move? After all, if the stock is sound, it is not going to go any lower than it does when everyone is trying to sell it. This illustrates how much you need to think for yourself when trading — if you follow the crowd, you might just be doing the opposite of what you should.

You can also try to understand the psychology behind a spike in the volume when the price is rising. Following the same logic, you may want to take your profit while the price is supported by so many buyers. Again, you need to review whether there is any underlying reason for the interest, which could suggest that the stock price will continue to rise instead. Look for the latest news releases about the company.

If you see a breakout, you may want to check the volume of trading associated with it, to see whether there is sentiment behind the move. A high volume on one or two days is called a "volume spike" and often signals the end of a trend, either up or down. A change in volume downward can also signal an end to a trend — all the people who wanted to sell have done so, and people who want to buy are not yet, as the price does not suit them. Expect that this situation will get resolved when either the bulls decide that the price is not so bad, or bearish sentiment lowers the price — in either case, there will be an increased volume to accompany the movement up or down.

ON-BALANCE VOLUME (OBV)

On-Balance Volume (OBV) is an indicator that brings together volume and price changes. It is a single line, which rises and falls, together with the price. When it moves in the opposite direction to the price, then that means to watch out. The divergence in direction between the two means that a change may be coming (this is a general principle with many indicators).

OBV was invented by Joe Granville and tracks whether buying is in support of a price rise or fall. It simply adds the volume of the day if the closing price is higher and subtracts the volume if it is lower. Effectively, that means it attributes all the buying on an up day to enthusiasm for the price, and all the volume on a down day to the bears selling — not particularly accurate, but it seems to work in practice.

A variation on this indicator is credited to Marc Chaikin, who thought that a more representative amount would come from considering whether the closing price was over the midpoint price for the day — this would add to the indicator. The opposite would take away from the indicator. His indicator, called Chaikin, is a smoother form of the OBV.

MOVING AVERAGE

The idea behind the moving average is simple, and you will find it used in many variations and in many ways by traders.

Put simply, a moving average is a way to smooth out the daily ups and downs of the market and try to determine any underlying trends. It is made up by adding together the prices, usually the closing prices, for the last X number of days and dividing by X. For each new day, the first price, now X+1 days ago, is dropped and the new price added to the calculation. It goes one stage beyond the trend lines we discussed earlier, as it is not limited to a straight line and changes dynamically with the stock. However, these changes are lagging the current action, so it may still be moving upward while the stock crashes and burns.

You obviously do not get involved in adding the prices together and dividing — this is a standard charting function that you will find on your broker's Web site and in custom-trading software. You can get several varieties of moving average, depending on how far back you go. The 20-day moving average, and other shorter periods, is often used for trading; you can also get 50-day and 200-day moving averages, which are of more use in detecting underlying long-term trends. The shorter the period, the closer the average is to the current price and the less the line is smoothed out. Some techniques involve using moving averages for a couple of different periods and comparing them. That will be covered later.

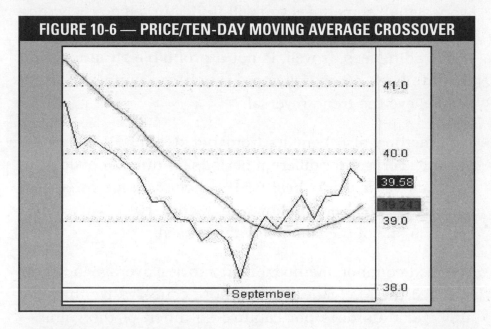

FIGURE 10-6 — PRICE/TEN-DAY MOVING AVERAGE CROSSOVER

The first method of using the moving average is the crossover method. Put simply, this uses the price crossing over the moving average line to signal when a change is coming. Consider Figure 10-6. When the price is falling, the moving average is falling but lagging behind the drop, so the prices are below the moving average line. When the prices start rising, they cross the line, and this gives a buy signal. As you can see, this identifies a change in trend fairly early on and so provides what you are seeking for trading success.

The crossover method also gives us the sell signal. In the opposite case to that above, when the price falls back below the line, we have started a downward trend and should sell and possibly buy the stock short. Of course, if it were that easy, then traders would stop their search for better indicators and just make money. Sometimes you will find that the price breaks through the line only to drop back in a day or two, giving you a false signal. If you trade on every signal, sometimes you will find yourself on the wrong side and wanting to buy back stock you just sold, which, with trading fees as well, is not a profitable situation. You should check other indicators, such as volume, to see if you believe the trend reversal.

This method also benefits from backtesting. You can try moving averages for different periods, or number of days, to see what value works best for the stock you are interested in trading. The period shown in Figure 10-6 is ten days, which is one of the common values used.

The next common method for the moving average indicator is called the level rule. This is more conservative than the first and thus does not capture so much of the gains — however, it is less likely to give a false signal and so may save some of the false moves. The moving average level rule says that you trade when the moving average for today changes from the direction it was going yesterday. For instance, if the moving average was going up each day, in an upward price trend, and today it is down from yesterday's number, then it signals that the uptrend has ceased, and you should sell and buy short.

As this is a lagging indicator, it is obvious that the price must have been falling already for this to happen, so it is not good at getting the best timing — however, it does reduce the false signals and excess trading. You can see in Figure 10-6 that the signal point would have been a few days later, but this might have avoided a fallback in the price.

The moving average works, but there are some problems with it. One problem is that not all stocks are trending all the time. If a stock is not moving up and down, then the moving average will be horizontal and no good as a trading tool. Having said that, common sense tells us that a stock that does not move up and down is not one that you want to consider much if you are trying to profit from trading, so you should just forget it and move on to consider another. Another problem has been mentioned above — getting false signals from movement outside the range.

Depending on the stock, this may be problematic. Some stocks are quite regular in their price range, and some vary widely — they are said to be more volatile, a concept we will cover more later. These would generate more false signals by crossing the moving average more often. You could compensate for this by deciding on further rules, such as the price must cross the line and stay crossed for a number of days before you trade. You have to decide on your own compromise between jumping on the trend in good time for a profit and trading too much by following a sensitive indicator.

You can change the number of days that you use in the moving average to try and achieve a balance between detecting the trends in time for a good profit and the danger of overtrading and losing your gains in costs and reversals.

SUCCESS BULLETS

- Patterns of prices are repeated across times and different stocks and can be recognized to detect trading points.

- Price uptrends may be punctuated by periods of consolidation, where the price remains the same.

- The triangle or pennant presages a breakout.

- The downward sloping flag may also be seen in an uptrend.

- One of the simplest reversal patterns is the double-bottom, where support is proven twice before an uptrend.

- Volume is a strong indicator and should be checked to verify an apparent breakout.

- The on-balance volume indicator combines volume and price in one indicator.

- Moving average crossover provides a simple if limited indicator of when to trade.

WORDS TO KNOW

Consolidation, cup-with-handle, double-bottom, flag, head-and-shoulders, moving average, pennant, reversal pattern, triangle

11

SOME BELLS & WHISTLES

OTHER TYPES OF MOVING AVERAGE

There are ways of creating a more complex indicator that is related to the ordinary moving average (or simple moving average, as it is called) but which tries to take account of the problems mentioned and produce better trading signals.

The first we should consider is the weighted moving average. This biases the value in favor of the newest numbers, which then have more effect on the current value. As noted above, the shorter the period of the moving average, the sooner the signal to trade. What the weighted moving average does is make the recent prices more significant, thus emphasizing the current movement and capturing the early signs of an opportunity.

Another variation is the exponential moving average. The calculation of this is not easy, and most charting programs will do it for you. The result of the calculation minimizes the difference between the moving average and the current price, which makes it more representative of latest prices, for similar reasons as expressed above.

Finally, there is also a family of moving averages called

adaptive moving averages. Again, these are calculated by your graphing program, and the effect is to reduce the impact of outlying values but still retain sensitivity to recent prices.

All these variations have been invented to try and improve the predictability of the future price changes. It is important that you realize that none of them is perfect and that you have to decide for yourself the significance that you want to place on them in your own trading system. Practicing reading what they tell you and backtesting are two key activities you should undertake to determine where the indications from moving averages fit into your style of trading.

MULTIPLE MOVING AVERAGES

There are advantages and disadvantages to short-period moving averages and to longer-term moving averages. The short-term moving averages are quicker at indicating a change in the market but may be too quick on a false move; the longer-term moving averages get around the errors of the short but are slow to respond and signal a buy. That is why you may want to juggle with the period of the moving average you use and even adjust it between different stocks.

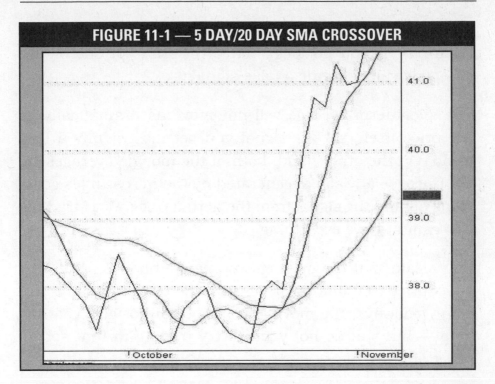

FIGURE 11-1 — 5 DAY/20 DAY SMA CROSSOVER

One idea generated from this dilemma is to plot two moving averages with different periods and take your signals from when the averages cross each other. You can see that this is just an extension of the crossover method, which triggers when the price crosses the moving average — the price is just a one-day moving average, after all.

Commonly, five days (a week) and 20 days (a month) are the periods chosen for the moving averages, although you are free to experiment with these numbers to try to refine the system. When the shorter moving average crosses to above the longer term — as in a price-crossing — it signals that you may want to buy, as the stock is rising. The opposite is of course true. When the short-term average crosses to below the long-term moving average, this signals that the price is falling and you want to sell and perhaps buy short.

There are advantages to this method. As you can see from Figure 11-1, you no longer have the issue of one or two renegade values giving a false signal.

The short-term average will not move as dramatically as the price itself, so any signal you get may signify a true trend. On the other hand, both of the moving averages lag the price, so any signal generated by their crossing is going to lag behind the signal from the actual price. With trading, you cannot have everything.

Note again that the moving average methods depend on a stock price trending up or down. If the price is steady, just going sideways, the moving averages cannot give you any help — but you do not want to try trading in that sort of stock anyway.

MOVING AVERAGE CONVERGENCE/DIVERGENCE (MACD)

All this discussion leads us to another indicator that was dreamed up to overcome perceived shortcomings of the previous methods. This goes by the grand name of moving average convergence/divergence indicator, or MACD for short, and was invented by Gerald Appel. It may be available on charting software, where it will thankfully be called by its acronym.

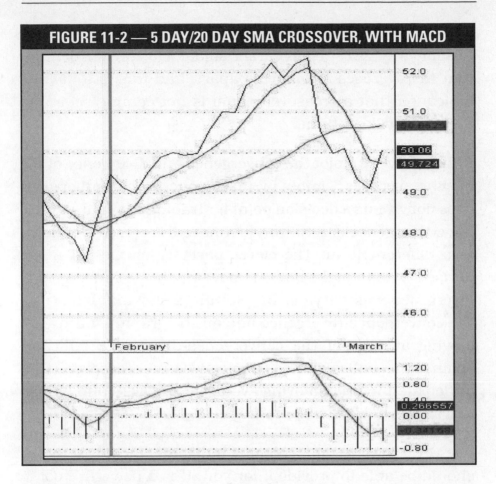

FIGURE 11-2 — 5 DAY/20 DAY SMA CROSSOVER, WITH MACD

As suggested by the name, this is based on moving averages again, but it takes the consideration of them one stage further, by gauging the convergence or divergence of the two moving average lines to or from each other. The previous section described the crossing of the lines as a signal point; this indicator takes it one step further and measures the rate at which they come together or drift apart.

The idea is that the crossing point of two moving averages, which may be taken as a signal to buy or sell, is inevitably going to lag the best point at which a trade should have been entered. However, before the averages cross, they must have converged on each other, so using convergence in some way gives us an earlier signal. Divergence denotes that the averages are moving apart, and this is a definite indication that a crossover signal is not coming soon and the trend will continue.

Although we can plot the convergence and divergence of the moving averages, simply by taking one from another, this does not give us a decision point for trading. If you wait until the convergence is zero, you just have the crossover shown in a different form. The clever part, which Gerald Appel devised, was to make obvious how much the convergence-divergence was varying, by plotting a moving average of the convergence-divergence line on the graph. Plotting the moving average of the convergence-divergence indicator against the indicator itself then gives us crossovers that anticipate the price-moving average crossovers and almost magically show us when to trade.

The MACD has become a popular indicator, and any software should be able to provide it for you. It is a powerful tool in your arsenal, and you should try to become well acquainted with it and able to interpret its moves at a glance. Like any indicator, market moves may happen that mislead it so it gives a wrong indication, but understanding the derivation of it and the fundamental principles that make it function will give you a way to explore whether the signals are real enough that you can act on them.

BOLLINGER BANDS

You now need to look at the concept of volatility in the stock price movement. For your purposes, you simply need to know that volatility means the amount that a stock price goes up and down. High volatility means that it moves a lot between high and low prices, and low volatility means that it is fairly stable and does not change much from day to day. The statisticians have more technical definitions that do not make much difference to our discussion of the principles. How you view and use volatility depends on what sort of trader you want to be — a volatile price may provide opportunities for short-term holding, but chasing a trend in a volatile stock can increase your chances of loss, as you might decide to get out of the stock because of a wild swing downward that was only a glitch on the way up.

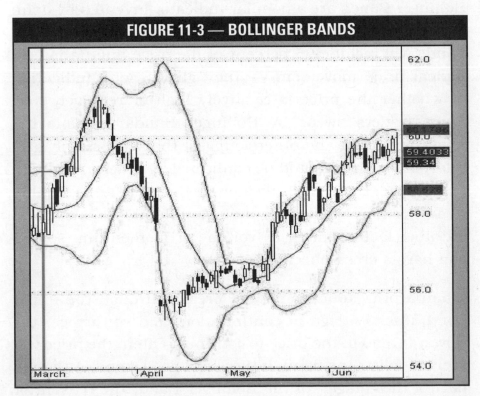

FIGURE 11-3 — BOLLINGER BANDS

These charts will be beginning to look quite familiar to you, but using Bollinger Bands is another twist on lines bracketing a stock price over time. Bollinger Bands are lines drawn on the chart to try to define what prices are high and what are low. They are based on a 15-day (by default) moving average, which is the middle line, or band, near the price. The volatility factor is worked in by drawing lines on each side at a distance of two standard deviations from the base. Standard deviation is a statistical term that puts a value on the amount of fluctuation. The exact derivation will not concern us, as it is all taken care of in the charting software.

Bollinger Bands are a popular indicator invented by John Bollinger. Statistics say that the two standard deviation bands will include 95 percent of the price fluctuation for typical price movement — they give a good indication of whether the price is relatively high or relatively low. Some traders swear by Bollinger Bands as almost a magic indicator, and others suggest that they simply give information that should be confirmed by other indicators. As Bollinger Bands already include the trend and volatility of a price, any confirming indicator should be one based on other factors, such as volume or momentum, so you can have a cross-checking system.

When a price touches or just breaks through the upper band, this is a sign of continuation, and you expect the upward trend in the price to continue. Often, the price will seem to follow the band, if there is a good trend. Although part of the "magic" of the Bollinger Band, the reason for this is obvious. The middle band is a moving average, which on an uptrend must always be below the price. The upper band is above this and thus likely to be around the current price.

The corollary of this is that when the price stops following the upper band, the trend upward is running out of steam. If the price turns downward, you may also see that the price tracks with the lower band, in a similar way to the upward case.

There is another way in which Bollinger Bands provide information, and that is by looking at the width between the upper and lower bands. If this range reduces, it may show that traders are not pushing or testing the price so much and may indicate a breakout is coming; however, the price may not reverse, and so you need to look for other indicators.

John Bollinger himself has said, "Tags of the bands are just that, tags, not signals. A tag of the upper Bollinger Band is not in and of itself a sell signal. A tag of the lower Bollinger Band is not in and of itself a buy signal."

MOMENTUM

Momentum is a measure of the speed of movement — in this case, of a price move. One of its uses is to have an indication of whether a stock is "overbought" or "oversold," that is, whether the market is losing steam in the existing trend. It is often used to confirm a decision from another indicator, and because it is from a different concept, it can provide a good check on other signals. There are several indicators derived from a stock's momentum — one has already been covered with the MACD. The Relative Strength Indicator

(RSI) and Stochastic Oscillator are other variations that are momentum-based, which will be examined later.

You may hear the term "momentum trader." Momentum in this case is more on the lines of Newton's First Law, roughly translated from the Latin as "Every object in a state of uniform motion tends to remain in that state of motion unless an external force is applied to it." The momentum trader uses this idea by jumping on a stock that is rising in price in the hope that it continues to do so. These are of necessity traders with a short time horizon, and the brief description does not do justice to the amount of thought that some of them put into their business. However, this is a different concept from the family of momentum indicators that we are considering and that are used in technical analysis.

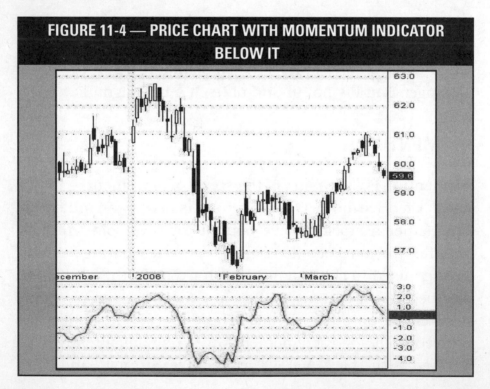

FIGURE 11-4 — PRICE CHART WITH MOMENTUM INDICATOR BELOW IT

Momentum is often calculated by comparing the price 10 days previously with the current price. With no change in price, the indicator will be at zero; the indicator shows the rate of change of price. When you plot the momentum indicator above or below the price bar chart, you can observe the usefulness. If a momentum indicator is represented by a horizontal line on the day in question, it does not mean that the price is not moving. It shows that the price is moving, up or down depending whether the line is above or below zero, at the same rate as ten days ago.

A rising slope on the momentum indicator line implies that the price is rising more strongly than previously and is an indication that it will continue to rise. You may take the crossing of the zero line as a buy or sell indicator (depending whether it is crossing upward or downward). Understanding the momentum-based indicator is a useful discipline, as it may appear to echo the trend of the stock price but is disconnected from it. The trend may be up or down, and the momentum indicator may also be up or down, or a horizontal line, if the price is increasing or decreasing at a steady rate.

RELATIVE STRENGTH INDICATOR

The Relative Strength Indicator (RSI), or Index, is one of the refinements that has been invented to improve the predictions from momentum. The idea is that it may give an earlier signal and provides reinforcement for that decision. Waiting for the momentum indicator to cross the zero line may delay getting into the trade, but if instead you take your signal as the change in direction of the momentum indicator without waiting for the cross-over, on the assumption that the move will continue, you risk the move running out of steam. The RSI tackles this objection by tracking the average up move compared with the average down move and ensuring that it is greater or that the momentum is relatively higher for the upward move. This indicates a stronger move that is more likely to continue.

The RSI uses the average upward move compared with the average downward move over a period of days, often 14. It is then mathematically put on a scale of 0 percent to 100 percent, although it will seldom be at the ends of this range, as it is based on averages. Any time it is over 70-75 percent, the stock is considered overbought and worth considering selling. If it is below 25-30 percent, the stock is oversold and may be bargain priced. These ideas are best compared with and confirmed by other indicators.

In a more detailed look at the RSI, the time to be especially alert is when the RSI is moving in an opposite direction to the stock price. If the stock price is rising or steady but the RSI starts downward from its high level, this may mean that the price will soon fall and is called a bearish divergence. Similarly, a bullish divergence is when the RSI starts to move up before the price does.

As a final note, the RSI is not to be confused with relative strength, which is a term used when comparing a stock with its market sector or index. RSI does not compare the stock with any other, only with itself.

STOCHASTIC OSCILLATOR

Another momentum-based indicator that you may find in your charting software is the Stochastic Oscillator. An oscillator in the trader's jargon is a device for indicating overbought/oversold events. The RSI is an oscillator, and you can see why it has this name, as it cycles up and down, providing information both by its value and by its movement.

The Stochastic Oscillator was invented by Dr. George Lane and was used a lot in the 1990s, when it became the holy grail for traders. It is of course just another manipulation of the numbers, so it does not possess magical properties, although it is powerful. The interesting point about this indicator is that it goes into more depth on the price movement than many others, considering the various values of each individual day bar.

The mechanics of its calculation are, thankfully, taken care of by a computer; however, you need to appreciate the concept of the Stochastic Oscillator, so we make no apology for explaining it here. The principle is comparing a stock's closing price to the whole range of prices that has been seen in time. As a price rises in an upward trend, the closing prices tend to be in the higher part of the range of prices. When the price is sinking, the closing prices tend to be near the bottom of recent price ranges. We use the names %K for the actual oscillator line and %D for the signal line, which is a smoothed out version of the oscillator.

The period of numbers considered may be specified and is commonly taken as 14 days. The calculation involves the closing price, say C, the lowest low in the last 14 days (L), and the highest high in the same period (H). Then

$$\%K = 100 \text{ x } (C\text{-}L)/(H\text{-}L)$$

You can see that %K is a percentage of how far up the recent range of prices the closing price is.

$$\%D = 3\text{-period moving average of }\%K$$

Technically, this is called a fast Stochastic. There is another version, preferred by some, which is imaginatively called the slow Stochastic. The slow Stochastic uses the calculation for %D as its %K, with the new slow %D being the 3-period moving average of the new %K. The slow Stochastic plots as a smoother line, which generates fewer and more reliable signals, but the signals lag behind the fast Stochastic signals.

In use, the guideline used is that a stock is overbought if the oscillator is above 80 percent, and oversold if it goes below 20 percent. Some traders take as their signal for buying the point at which the oscillator moves from below to above 20 percent, and above to below 80 percent for a sell signal. Others look for the crossing of the %D line, the moving average. When the lines are below 20 percent and %K crosses from below to above %D, that triggers the buy signal. If the lines are above 80 percent, and the %K drops below the %D, then is the time to sell. These decision points, as always, should be supported by other indicators based on other factors before trading. You can also look for divergences between the oscillator and the price, as described in the RSI section, as this can be a powerful prediction tool.

AVERAGE DIRECTIONAL MOVEMENT INDEX (ADX)

The Average Directional Movement Index is part of a system developed by Wells Wilder, and it is designed to show the strength of the price movement. It does not indicate the direction of the movement, so it must be used in conjunction with other factors. Commonly it appears along with the +DI and the -DI indicators in the charting software.

The +DI is the Plus Directional Indicator, and the -DI is the Minus Directional Indicator. These are often 14-day indicators, which are lines that move in opposite directions. Each one measures the current period's range compared with the previous period's range. If you use just these indicators, you would normally buy when +DI rises above -DI, and sell when +DI goes below -DI. As they move around a lot, this can result in overtrading.

The ADX will help with that. The ADX is the difference between the +DI and the -DI as an exponential indicator. The ADX scale goes up to 100, and anything above 30 is taken as an indication of a trend. However, unlike most other indicators, rising does not necessarily mean a buy signal; it could equally well signal a sell.

To use these indicators together, you want to be in the market only when ADX is greater than 30, as below 30 indicates that the stock is not trending. You can then use the indication from the crossing of the +DI and -DI for your signal, and the ADX will tend to keep you out until there is a real trend and reduce the chance of overtrading. So if the ADX goes above 30 and +DI is going in the same direction, crossing -DI, that is a buy signal. Note that if the ADX goes above 30, and -DI is following in the same direction, this is a signal to go short on the stock. You would get out of your position if the ADX reduced below 30 or if the spread between the DIs reduced.

A variation on this combination is given by Barbara Star, in *Secrets of Successful Traders*. She suggests using the MACD to determine the direction of the trend, in conjunction with the ADX indicating the strength. An uptrend is indicated by both indicators rising together, and a downtrend or shorting opportunity when the indicators diverge, with the MACD heading downward.

SUCCESS BULLETS

- Multiple moving averages give a signal where they cross which lags the moving average and price crossover signal but is less prone to false triggering.

- The MACD indicator provides earlier signals of pending changes in the trend by measuring the convergence of moving averages.

- Bollinger Bands show whether prices are relatively high or low. A narrowing between the bands may indicate a breakout is coming.

- The momentum indicator shows you the rate of change of price, and crossing the midpoint provides a buy/sell indication.

- The Relative Strength Indicator and Stochastic Oscillator are momentum based and show if stocks are overbought or oversold.

- The Average Directional Movement Index shows the strength of price movement and needs to be used with other indicators for price direction.

WORDS TO KNOW

Average Directional Movement Index (ADX), Bollinger Bands, momentum indicator, Moving Average Convergence/Divergence (MACD), Relative Strength Indicator (RSI), Stochastic Oscillator

12

MANAGING THE SWING

Back in Chapter 5, we discussed the type of trading that you were going to concentrate on. Although we covered the distinctions in types of trading, the term swing trader is used fairly generally for those who seek to make an income in the market, and commonly it refers to people who trade in periods from day to a week or two. Those who focus on trading as a full-time job are usually called day traders and do not often hold positions overnight. On the other hand, traders who place weight on value analysis, as well as technical analysis, are called position traders and are on the longer-term part of the trading spectrum. The basics of technical analysis spelled out here are applicable to both day and swing trading. Both types of moneymaking are looking for short-term movements or swings in stock prices.

YOUR TRADING PLAN

Although previous chapters have covered many of the traditional indicators and demonstrated their use, you may have noticed that a specific step-by-step plan by which you will profit on the market has not been presented. The purpose of this chapter is not to give you a finished plan to create profits but to show you how you should go about preparing your own plan and developing it. You see, if I gave a system in this book, it would not be suitable for everyone. You need to develop a system that fits in with your personality and your schedule, as well as appealing to your psychology — the only way to score a real edge over other traders is to keep developing your own system.

There is no universal best method to picking the stocks; no one size fits all. If you read the Case Studies in this book, you will see that discipline is one of the most important aspects to being able to consistently profit, and we will come back to that later. But to have a methodology where you can exercise discipline, you must first prepare your plan. Without a plan, you will be lost in the wide world of stocks, not knowing where to start or how to proceed. The professional traders all seem to favor simplicity but have hard-earned experience that they use with other factors to confirm their moves. You must figure out for yourself the direction that your trading life will take.

There are many trading systems on the market, each touted as the best thing ever. Each may be able to teach you something, but none can substitute for you doing your own homework and deriving a system that suits your personality and desired method of trading. The only problem is that it can take much work to make a system from scratch. You might want to start with a good system and work on refining it. In trading you are essentially pitting your knowledge and observation against other traders — the underlying value of a stock is fairly constant in the times that we are considering and will rarely change as quickly as we need to make a profit, so when we profit we are scoring from others' mistaken trades — from them selling the stock that is about to rise, for instance.

What constitutes a trading system is open to debate. Some will depend on a simple indicator such as the moving average crossover to buy, with a stop-loss in place in case the expected increase in price does not happen. This may be the simplest example of a mechanical trading system, which means that it forces the buy and sell with clear signals. You may also run across discretionary trading systems — these give you a heads up about certain programmed conditions being met but then leave the buying or selling decision to you. These are much more difficult to backtest in a meaningful manner, and, being subject to your experience and the emotions, may be best left alone for now.

The previous chapters on charts and indicators provide a good background to the world of stocks and are also applicable to other similar markets, such as Foreign Exchange (Forex). The following guidelines are appropriate for designing your own trading system for any similar exchanges. Bear in mind that however good your system is, you cannot expect that every trade will go your way — the trick to successful trading is to have your gains exceed your losses. Apart from choosing a stock that moves in the right direction, this can be achieved by setting tight stops to get you back out of the stock if it reverses on you and by choosing winning stocks that have the possibility of gaining more than the amount that you are prepared to lose on each losing trade.

CHOOSING YOUR STOCKS

When you are trading using technical analysis, a system that you are comfortable with is the most important factor. The exact stock that you use it on is a secondary consideration, as prices tend to behave in similar ways over all stocks. After all, all stocks are traded in the same way, with human beings deciding to buy and sell, whether directly in front of the screen or by pre-programmed responses, on all exchanges; you should expect similar results whichever you trade. That said, there are some differences. Some stocks might be subject to more volatility, for example, and you can use your system backtesting to throw out the stocks that do not seem to want to play by your rules.

The next part in developing your system is to narrow down the stocks that you are going to study. Despite the fact that you do not intend to stay in the stocks long-term, you want to pick stocks that are relatively large and in a strong sector. With more than 9,000 available, you cannot hope to get to know the vagaries of price movement of each, and it is not necessary.

You want to go for stocks that have good liquidity and high trading volumes, that is, are not a problem to buy and sell. This rules out many small "penny stocks," which may be better suited for the speculative investor than the swing trader. The only downside to trading the large stocks is that there are many other traders adopting the same guidelines, which may put some limit on the number and size of trading opportunities. You may want to look at stocks that are just outside the top ones, so that there will be less of a professional following and more chance of "dumb money" on the other side of your trades.

Another factor in selecting your stock is that it is easier to trade if the stock is in a trend — upward, if you are going long (buying the stock), or downward if you are shorting the stock. Often, this will be obvious from looking at the charts, and of course, you should make sure that you view the charts over the time periods that you are thinking of trading, as this will affect the efficiency of your trades.

GETTING OUT

Every trade that you place, before you place it, should have a clearly defined exit strategy. This means that, before you even enter the position, you must plan what to do if you get it wrong. Only in this way will you limit your losses so that you can succeed. The market is bigger than you. It is no good saying that something should have happened when it did not, as no amount of logic or justification will retrieve a loss that the market imposed on you. The most successful traders lose some, but they know how to prevent it becoming a catastrophe. It is said that if you achieve 70 percent of your trades going the right way, you are doing excellently. Of course, you also want the successful trades to continue upward to a much greater extent than the losers go downward, and the only thing under your direct control in that equation is to cut your losses short. The next chapter goes into detail about how to implement these judgments.

TREND-FOLLOWING TRADING

First, let us consider trend-following trading systems. One of the simplest examples of this was mentioned in the section on multiple moving averages. The use of the specific periods of five-day and 20-day moving averages is attributed to Richard Donchian. The signal to buy is when the five-day average crosses the 20-day average upward. The sell signal is a crossing in the other direction. This is about as simple as it gets.

Many trend systems are based on the simple moving average. You will find one difficulty with it, however — if the stock is not trending but moving around a steady value, you will get crossings almost at random, and you will be triggering lots of pointless trades that will eat up your resources. You can mechanize a test of this condition by checking for increases recently — for example, compare the price with a long-term average, or check that the moving average is rising. You will test different periods and comparisons when backtesting.

You may want to check on other criteria or indicators to validate the crossing, or to try to anticipate the crossing — you will recall that one disadvantage of using simple moving averages is that by their nature they lag the price movement, so that you may end up "leaving money on the table" with your late entry and late exit. However, be wary of adding too much complication to your system, as you then may have to deal with conflicting signals and other issues. One of the secrets of successful trading is to have a plan you can stick with, because when you introduce discretion, your personal feelings will not start influencing your decisions, perhaps detrimentally.

COUNTERTREND SYSTEMS

You can also trade successfully with the countertrend. For the new trader, this is not such a good choice, even though the countertrend idea of buying at the absolute low and selling high is the ultimate profit-taking strategy. The countertrend systems try to identify the point of trend reversal, also called inflection points. This can be done by reviewing the range or channel of the stock price but is far from guaranteed to work. If you pursue a countertrend system, you should ensure tight stops and also check for other indicators.

BREAKOUT TRADING

In Chapter 9, Support and Resistance, the idea of lines, called channels, which bracketed the movement of the stock price was addressed. The idea of a breakout going outside the lines and signaling a move to a new level was also introduced. A stronger indication of the breakout in this case is when the line breaks out and there is also a gap from the last price to the new breakout price. This suggests strong support for the change in price level.

This can be programmed in various ways and is a good candidate for testing to refine your margins. A simple move above the line, if it is significant (which can be checked by imposing a percentage overrule), may be a sufficient indication that the price has broken out; alternatively, you may program your system to detect a gap. Note that the gap is significant only if it occurs outside the channel but that it is usually important when it does and is more strong than a simple move out of the range.

These indications are best checked by other factors. If the typical trading volume changes at the same time, this is a further indication that the breakout has some significance. You may check that the breakout is still there at the close of the day, as this means more than crossing the line during the day; you can also build in a delay, so that one or two days over the line can be ignored, unless the move continues.

The breakout gives only a buy signal, so you will need to put in place a good strategy for selling at a profit. You do not want to wait for another channel to be established and a breakout to the downside before selling, as you will leave significant gains behind. This highlights another issue with proving your trading system — you may need to adjust entry and exit formulas independently to derive the best gains. The wealth of choices that you have for your system is the reason that it will take you some time and effort to refine your thoughts through backtesting, but you will be learning all the time and will know that the result is your personal creation.

TRADING VOLATILITY

Volatility is a key difference between the value or fundamental analysis trader and the swing trader. Volatility is not wanted when you are seeking stocks that will steadily increase in price to match the value that your research has shown, to your satisfaction, is the correct level for them. If anything, volatility will just get you jittery about whether you made the right move. On the other hand, swing traders may exploit volatility to advantage, and, at least, appreciate the ability of the stock to make quick moves for fast profits. Volatility does indicate degree of riskiness. This is something that the technical trader learns to deal with and the value investor does not appreciate.

Look back at the Chapter 11 section on Bollinger Bands, which are perhaps the most well-known indicator embracing volatility. Notice that, as in the previous section, these give you upper and lower price bands from which you can figure breakout movement. Again, you can backtest and play with the period over which the Bands are calculated, to see what best fits the stock, or category of stocks, that you are interested in.

Swing traders are interested in high-volatility stocks, because there is more opportunity for profit if you read the situation correctly. There is a factor called historic volatility, which is available on charting software, which gives you a good indication of how much the stock price fluctuates. As volatile stocks seem to quiet down just before a breakout, this is another factor that you can figure into your plan. This is signaled by the narrowing of the width between the Bollinger Bands, as mentioned in that section. Bollinger Bands give you a great deal of scope for developing a system and have been the basic building block for many a successful trading plan.

TRADING RANGE-BOUND

Rather than waiting for a breakout move in your chosen stocks, you can also trade within a range that has been established. If you have a clearly defined range, you will know the upper and lower limits that you can expect, even in a trending stock where the average value is increasing. Barring a breakout, you can repeatedly buy at the lower line and sell at the higher line, making a series of small profits that in sum far exceed the average growth of the stock.

Be warned that this is like countertrend trading, something that you need to be careful about when you are inexperienced. It is easy to see where the range was after the fact, but to identify it accurately in real time while it is still valid takes some experience and a little guesswork. In this case, you are also less likely to get worthwhile assistance from your software. As you are also aiming to make repeated small gains, you must also be aware of your commission costs, as they will eat into any hypothetical profits.

The approach is similar to breakout trading, except in this case you expect that the price will keep oscillating in the channel and not break out. You may buy using a limit price just above the support line and expect that the price will rise back up. Your stop-loss order would be below the support line, with a small margin, so as not to sell on a brief fluctuation but protect you from a downward breakout.

TRADING PULLBACKS

A pullback is where a price temporarily stops rising or drops in a fundamentally rising trend. It is considered a consolidation of the position. If you want to trade the pullback, all you have to do is buy the stock when the price stops declining and starts going up, following the underlying trend. Technically you would get into this by placing a stop order just above the high price of the previous day's trading. If the pullback continued on the next day, the order would not be filled, and you would have another opportunity to do the same thing again. If the pullback ceased and the stock started to rise, then the condition of the order would be met and your purchase would go ahead. You should then immediately place a stop-loss order to sell if the price dropped below the previous day's lowest price and each day revise this to protect your gains.

STOPPING OUT

An essential part of your trading plan is to know when you are going to sell your stocks. Known as "stopping out," this is the point where all those gains become real (or where you prevent further losses). Some stops are self-adjusting as the stock price moves with time, and some you can know in advance.

The first principle is to set a stop as soon as you get into a position. This is your protection against losing too much if the stock price turns against you. Do not fall for the thought that you are going to keep an eye on the price and have a stop level in mind. This is the way many traders become losing traders. They justify their hesitation to close out the position by reanalyzing the stock, but they are just succumbing to their emotions. In setting the initial stop, the considerations that you have to have for this are:

- If this stop is set too close to your entry price, then the stock, which may otherwise be a good choice, may dip slightly and trigger a sale before it runs up. This is frustrating, as you can imagine, because you are down a small amount on the price, down for the trading costs, and you made a correct stock selection from which you did not profit.

- If the stop is set too low, then a stock that genuinely moved the wrong way would not be sold until you had lost more than you needed to and thus did not protect your trading capital as well as you might have.

Regarding the principle of preserving your capital, it would be wise to set the size of your trade no larger than that which would result in a 1 to 2 percent loss on your account. This is important for two reasons:

- When you have only this much at risk, you are better able to control your emotions and stick with your proven (after testing) system to control the trade.

- If your losses run higher than this, it takes only a certain amount of bad luck and your account could be decimated, which is a difficult situation from which to recover.

As part of your testing of the system, try changing the amount by which you set the initial stop. You will see some winning trades stopped out too soon, and you may even find this is inevitable in honing your system. You should be able to find an optimum level for best return over the years of testing data, which you can then incorporate in your system. Know also that different stocks and different markets exhibit different levels of volatility, and the level that you set the stop at has to take this into account, as it will plainly affect the early stop-out problem. Rigorous testing is the key to developing faith in your system so that you will follow its rules and not try to second-guess it.

Some of the entry conditions given above have associated expected gains and thus are more easy cases for which to choose an exit point. For instance, if you are going for range-bound trading, you would expect to sell when you approach the top of the range. Others, where you are following a trend upward, may not have an expected limiting value, and you need to look at adjusting your stop as the value increases to preserve your gains.

One of the fairly universal ways of getting out of a stock is with a trailing stop. These follow the rising price, at a set level below it, which can be either dollar or percentage based. They never go back down, so if the price drops, it approaches the stop level, and you sell the stock without losing too much of your gains. These have the same problem as the initial stop when trading highly volatile stocks — the price may fluctuate sufficiently to trigger the sale and then continue going upward. Only by experimentation can you determine what works best for the particular equity that you are considering. Even then, your testing will be accurate only for past events, although this may be the best that you can do — even volatility can change for a particular stock over time.

A refinement on this automatic trailing stop may be worthwhile; you can also set your stop in terms of the previous values. In a rising trend, you can reset your stop to reflect more accurately the levels that you do not expect it to return to. For instance, you can set it to the highest low that the market just made — assuming the next day is better, it will not come down to that level again. A strategy that is less likely to take you out of the stock early is to set the trailing stop to the previous highest low, giving a little wiggle room before you take your profit.

Another type of stop, or exit strategy, is given by using indicators. This is likely to give you less profit, as most indicators are lagging to some extent. The simple moving average is an example of a definite signal that will prevent you hanging on in hope, even if it does not signal at the peak. You would exit when the price crosses the moving average downward, and in this case many people use the ten-day moving average, although this is something with which you can experiment.

Another indicator-based stop is to exit the position if the stock price goes lower than the lowest price in the last three days, for example. Again, this is simple to program for backtesting and gives a definite signal that should not be ignored if you are working in a disciplined manner.

A third class of stop is time based. If the stock fails to

deliver within a certain time of holding it, there are several reasons that you might want to sell it. First, your money may do better invested in a different stock rather than staying around the same value indefinitely. Second, if the stock does not perform as you expected, the basis for your initial entry may be in question, and you may want to get out and get cash that you can use elsewhere rather than wait to see what the stock wants to do.

TESTING YOUR SYSTEM

Before you play in earnest, it is highly recommended that you test your system extensively. You need historical data for this, and there are a variety of sources. You can do a search on the Internet to find them. Some are free, such as MSN MoneyCentral, and some are paid services and may provide the data on CD as well as online. You should also check what is available with your trading software license.

The first step is entering your trading rules on your software. Incidentally, while you can do a lot with a spreadsheet, we recommend that you commit the investment to buy a purpose-built system solution, such as MetaStock and TradeStation. Then you should run your test over possibly ten years of data to see how your system would have performed.

What you do next depends on your system rules. You may want to test alternative time periods, if you have a moving average based system, and find if you can get any improvement. You have to realize that you are working with unique previous conditions, so trying to optimize the numbers is worthwhile to a certain extent but can be a waste of time if indulged in too extensively.

A method to test your optimization is to do your first tests using only part of the data. When you have "tuned" your system, repeat your backtesting using the other batch of data and see whether you have improved the results consistently.

Another point to watch when you are trying to refine your system by doing backtesting: examine your output, watch out for systems that "succeed" by making a few highly profitable trades, and rely on these for their score. It is likely that such a system will be disappointing in regular use. What you are looking for is sufficient evidence that your system works so that you will not be tempted to modify it in an ad hoc manner. That would bring emotion back into the equation and is almost invariably going to bring about failure.

After you have coded and tested your system, you can explore other factors that may affect your profitability. One of these might be assessing the downside risk and determining if the rules can be modified to reduce the impact of the wrong trades. Changing your stop-loss may help, and there will be an optimum where it is not so small that you get stopped out of a trade that swings back up or so large that you lose more than you need to before dumping the stock.

Having done this process on the first stock of interest, know that different stocks can react differently and that you should go through the same fine-tuning process for any other stocks in which you are interested. You may want to limit your active trading interest to about ten stocks so that you can keep up to date with their movements.

TRADING OTHER MARKETS

For simplicity, I have repeatedly referred to stocks when talking about your trading. Although this is a likely entry to your trading career as it is so universally accessible and understandable, the other financial instruments mentioned in Chapter 2 are also available and able to be traded. The principles discussed are applicable to any freely available market where people are buying and selling, as it is the reaction of the people that controls the movement of the prices.

FUTURES

These can be some of the most risky instruments to be involved with; they are a commitment, come what may, to buy or to sell something on a certain day at a certain price. Futures contracts can be made for stocks, currencies, or commodities; just about anything that can be traded can be traded in this manner. The futures markets are mainly used by traders to speculate and not so much for the end user of the product, if there is one — after all, the end user would make only one contract if he wanted to get the product, and traders will buy and sell the contracts several times before the due date.

The essence of a futures contract is that you can leverage

your money — you do not pay the full price for the commodity when you buy the contract but just pay a premium for the contract so you can profit or lose more than you pay out in the first place. This makes them volatile and a place where fortunes can be made or lost. The contract is binding and can be enforced under law.

Futures traders will talk about their "positions" in a contract. Having a "short position" means that you contract to sell the goods on the due date, that is, you are short of the goods. You would expect that the price is going down, so that you could buy more cheaply to satisfy the contract and make your profit. You do not have to buy the goods, as you will just sell the contract when you see the profit you want to take, but in theory you would have to.

If you are in a "long position," it means that you have agreed to buy the goods on the due date at a certain price. You are betting that the actual price will go up and that your contract will allow you to buy more cheaply than the actual market price on the day. Again, you will not deal with the goods.

OPTIONS

Options are similar to futures in that there is a contract for a sale by a specific date in the future. The big difference is that you have no obligation to buy the underlying security or product at that date — you can just let the option expire worthless, which, although it sounds a waste, is rather better than being caught on the hook for a sum of money, as you can be with futures.

Trading in options is a large topic and easily capable of filling this book. For that reason, we will go into the subject matter in some depth, so that you can decide whether this is the area you want to pursue, but you will need to do more research to deal in options with confidence. The most important feature of trading options is that it leverages your money — you do not have to spend enough to buy the stock or security to control it and benefit from its price moves.

Background

Options have been readily available for buying and selling only since 1973. In that year, the Chicago Board of Trade created a stock option exchange, the Chicago Board Options Exchange. At its opening, the CBOE (pronounced **see**-bo) traded call options for just 16 stocks and had fewer than 1,000 trades on the first day. Nowadays, CBOE trades options in more than 1,500 stocks and 100 stock indexes and handles about 50 percent of all options traded. Its average daily volume is more than 1,000,000 contracts. Each option contract is for 100 of the underlying shares, so that is a staggering 100,000,000 shares of daily trading volume.

Option Types

The world of option trading has its own jargon, and understanding it is essential to not getting into trouble quickly.

A call is the right to buy a particular stock at a set price at any time up to a certain date. A put is the right to sell the stock at a set price at any time up to a certain date.

You pay a premium for these rights, but you do not have to exercise, or go through with them, if the market price of the stock is not what you want.

The options game is a zero-sum game, other than commissions. When someone, called an option holder buys a call or a put, someone else is selling them, and the seller is called an option writer or option grantor. The actual stock price that is set is called the strike price or exercise price. The strike prices are typically at $5 intervals, although they may be $10 increments for expensive stocks and $2.50 increments for cheap stocks. Option exchanges will consider the liquidity when setting the intervals.

An important point, often forgotten by beginners but maybe only once, is that option prices are per share, and option contracts are for 100 shares.

Note that you can take a stance as an option writer and get paid for the option contract. However, if the option is exercised, you will have to come up with the goods, either finding the shares to respond to a call or buying the shares if it was a put. Thus you may lose money, but in the meantime you have received the premium for your risk. If the option holder does not exercise his or her rights, as the stock did not move as he or she thought and then the option expires, you are off the hook and just pocket the premium as profit.

When you buy the option, whether a call or a put, you are said to go long on the option. If you sell the option, you go short on the option. This means that you can be involved in option trading in four ways:

- Go long calls in the stock.

- Go long puts in the stock.

- Go short calls in the stock.

- Go short puts in the stock.

For the first two you will be paying the premium and getting the option; with the other two you receive the premium and will have to wait to see if the option is exercised, which may mean that you lose.

You may have heard about covered calls, which is one way to reduce your risk in certain circumstances. When you take up a covered call, it means that you buy the shares for which you are selling a call. You do two transactions. If the call is exercised by the option holder, you have to hand over your shares at the strike price — but as you already own them, you are not going to get caught out by a massive swing. If the call expires, you keep the premium, and you can even think about selling another contract and setting up another covered call.

Buying Options

With so much trading in options going on, you are able to find options for various months and strike prices on one particular stock. These will be priced according to the market's view of the risk/reward, so there can be many prices associated with one stock. The dates are set as the Saturday after the third Friday in a month — you can specify only the month when considering the expiration date. If the option is to be exercised, it has to be by the close on the third Friday.

An order for an option is a little more complex than the simple stock trading we have been looking at so far. In addition to specifying quantity and buy/sell, an option has to specify the stock, the month of expiration and whether you want a call or a put. You can use market orders but may employ limit orders to be sure of the price. The order, as with stocks, may never be filled, but if it is, it will be at a price equal to or better than that specified. An example would be to "Buy 3 IBM December 110 calls at 4." This would mean that you want to buy calls for 300 shares in IBM at a share price of $110, with an expiration date of the third Friday in December, at a price of $4 each or better. The cost is 300 x $4, or $1,200. If the price of IBM reaches $114 per share before the expiration, then you can break even (as it cost you $4 per share for the option). You can also use stop-loss orders to protect yourself from too great a loss.

An option is called "in the money" if the stock price is better than the strike price, that is, it is worth exercising the option, "out of the money" if the stock price is not good enough to make money on exercising the option, and "at the money" if the market price of the stock is at the strike price. Note that even if you are in the money, you might not have a profit, as the option would have cost you something to buy. You need the stock price to reach the strike price plus the cost of the option to break even (apart from trading costs).

As I stated at the start of the section, if you want get serious about trading options, you will have to do quite a lot more research. Options traders have in their armaments some exotic trading tools like the straddle or butterfly, and many other ways of trading. To give you a taste of the compound "bets" that are made when trading options, those particular ones are implemented as follows.

The straddle is taking both a call and a put on the same stock for the same date and strike price. Why would you do this? Because you think that the stock is becoming more volatile and about to break out of its current range, and no matter which way it breaks, you stand to win if it moves far enough by the expiration date. Your maximum loss happens if the underlying security is priced at exactly the strike price, and it gets better from there, regardless of which way the price breaks.

A butterfly gets a little more complex, by taking four options at three different prices. The butterfly trade is neutral, as you do not need to decide whether the stock is going up or down, you are more concerned about whether the stock price will move substantially or very little, and you buy your options accordingly. For example, a "long butterfly" looks for little movement, and can be executed with either calls or puts. With calls, you would purchase one call at the current price minus $5, one call at the current price plus $5, and sell two calls at the current price. From buying two calls and selling two calls, you may have a net debit. You profit whenever the price moves little (maximum profit is when the price hasn't changed), and does not go further than the upper or lower strike prices, less the net debit, by the date of expiration. You are essentially betting that the stock price will not move much.

These are just some of the many plays that are routinely made when dealing with options, and I think you will be able to see why learning about options is a substantial topic, needing further study and research. I hope I have been able to give you a reasonable idea about the whole system of trading options to determine whether it might be the type of trading into which you would like to look further.

SUCCESS BULLETS

- Swing traders are concerned with trading periods from days to several weeks.

- You are responsible for developing a trading plan to suit your individual circumstances and personality.

- You will narrow down the list of stocks that you are interested in trading so that you can backtest their behavior.

- You must have a defined exit strategy before entering a trade.

- With a trend-following system, you use indicators that may lag the price movement to signal the trade.

- A countertrend system tries to detect the inflection points, that is, the points at which the trend changes.

- Breakout trading uses the price breaking through a predetermined boundary to signal a significant move.

- Bollinger Bands show stock volatility and can be used with a breakout strategy.

- Range-bound trading relies on the price being well-behaved and not breaking out.

- To trade pullbacks you watch for consolidation and buy for the recommencement of the trend.

- Your exit point should risk a loss of only 1 percent to 2 percent and should be set as soon as you buy the stock.

- You should test your system with historical data to establish the parameters that suit you and the stock traded and develop confidence in the system.

- As well as stocks, you could consider trading futures and options.

WORDS TO KNOW

Call, covered call, exercise, option holder, option writer, premium, pullback, put, stopping out, strike price

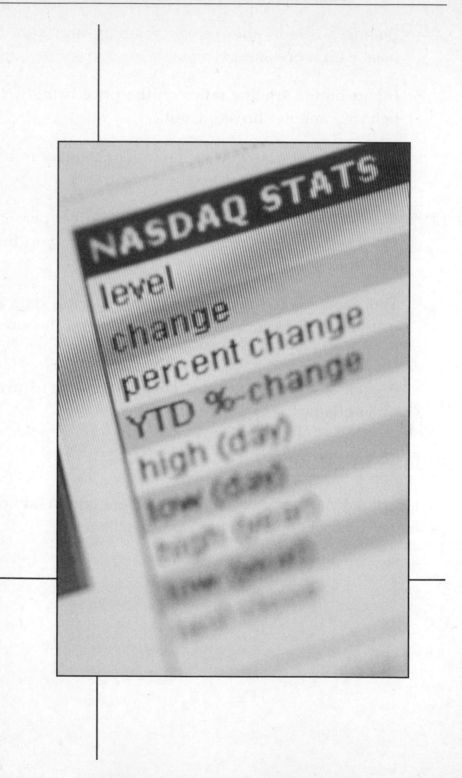

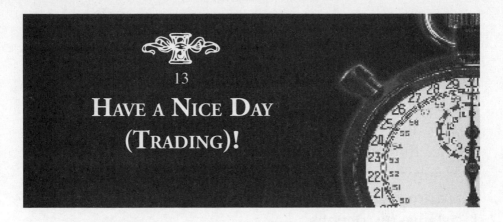

13

HAVE A NICE DAY
(TRADING)!

Many of the guidelines in the previous chapter also apply if you want to go into the more intensive world of day trading. There are some important regulatory as well as technical differences, which I will mention in this chapter.

First, day trading proper is about buying and selling stocks quickly when necessary, sometimes in seconds. To properly implement day trading, you need Level II access — anything else would be frustrating and maybe lose you money. Day trading is all about jumping in for a short time and taking a quick and not so large profit as often as you can. This is the video gaming world of trading.

Day traders buy in lots of 1,000 shares. To do any less would mean that slippage is significant and would render the whole exercise not worthwhile. However, you also need a lot of money to start day trading because of Federal Government regulations. You will be considered a "pattern day trader," and you are required to maintain $25,000 in your account at each end of day. Day traders are "flat," or out of the market each day, and do not hold any stocks overnight. Subject to your broker approval, your margin account can be four times the amount that you deposit, so this gives you a remarkable ability to get yourself into financial trouble if you are not prudent with your trading.

When day trading, you will seldom have time for the luxury of studying the stocks' fundamentals. However, you should take time to establish some basic facts about the stocks that you will be following so that you do not get any surprises. Your main issues with this sort of trading, apart from choosing the appropriate time to buy, are the legislative restrictions.

It is said that it takes six months to learn how to day trade successfully, and, if you are not trading successfully during that time, by definition you are losing money. You must be diligent in establishing strict money control so that you limit your losses, otherwise you will be broke before you can profit from your experience. Most traders recommend immediately entering a stop-loss order as soon as you get into a trade. That is good advice that also counts in swing trading but is ten times more important in day trading. Also, your trade should have an expected or hoped for profit level, and you will want to be clear on this before you even enter the trade. Otherwise, you run the risk of hesitation after you see the increase and the price dropping back before you can realize your profits. When entering a position, it is quite common to place a limit order for buying the shares, as the last thing you want is to pay over your expected price to buy stocks on which you do not expect to make a big profit.

Having said that day trading is fast paced, you should not make it so if the conditions are not there. Just because you are trading quickly, or a lot, does not mean that you should be able to make money if only you were experienced enough. There are times when the right trade is not there. It does not hurt to wait for the right conditions, but it certainly does hurt to buy in the wrong conditions.

Another way to harm your account is to hesitate after the right conditions are there. This allows other traders, who are not so retiring, to jump on the trade, to change the values in front of your eyes, and make the trade unprofitable. It is no good trying to chase the train when it has left the station, and chasing after a trend is similarly not a good plan.

It should go without saying that you need to be aware of the timing of your bodily functions, and be careful to be in a situation to close out your positions at any time when you have to leave your computer unmonitored. The nature of day trading means that seconds and minutes certainly count, and you need to be set up with snacks and drinks before you even get going in the morning so that you can give the screen your full attention without breaks for as long as possible.

Toni Turner is experienced in all types of trading, and writes extensively about trading. In the Case Study that follows, she talks of her earlier experiences and development.

SUCCESS STORY: TONI TURNER

Toni Turner is a trader/investor with 17 years of experience. She is the best-selling author of *A Beginner's Guide to Day Trading Online, A Beginner's Guide to Short-Term Trading*, and *Short-Term Trading in the New Stock Market*. Her books have been translated into Vietnamese, Japanese, and Chinese. She is a popular educator and speaks at trading forums and financial conferences across the United States.

Toni has appeared on NBC, MSNBC, CNN, and CNBC. She has been interviewed on dozens of radio programs and featured in periodicals such as *Fortune* magazine, *Stocks and Commodities, SFO, MarketWatch, Fidelity Active Trader*, and *Bloomberg Personal Finance*.

Toni is the President of TrendStar Trading Group, Inc. For more information, go to: **www.ToniTurner.com**

What types of trading are you involved with?	I mainly trade equities and ETFs (exchange-traded funds). I trade and invest in all times, intraday, swing, position, and long-term. So, you could say that depending on the market environment, I hold positions from two minutes to two years.
How did you start trading?	I started trading in the mid-1990s. Because I was an active and successful investor, I assumed trading would be "a walk in the park." Wow! Was I wrong! My first two day trades were highly profitable and definitely can be attributed to beginner's luck. The trades made $3 and $7 per share, respectively. I quickly grabbed my gains, and I thought I was a genius. Next, I maxed out my account — margin and all — on a stock in which the underlying company was going to solve the world's Y2K problems. The day after I bought it, the stock dropped 12 points. I remember sitting at my computer, watching in horror as my position — and much of my account — dissolved. I was too paralyzed with fear and inexperience to sell the position. In the background, I heard CNBC news anchor Joe Kernen say he'd never seen a stock fall that far, that fast.

SUCCESS STORY: TONI TURNER	
	The next two years were definitely not a walk in the park! The Y2K stock, plus a host of additional "more guts than brains" losses were a tough initiation into the world of trading. Still, I persisted, determined to fight my way back to profitability. I immersed myself in the markets, studied technical analysis and market mechanisms nonstop, and traded every day. After about two years, I recouped my losses and began to see consistent profits.
What are your likes and dislikes about trading?	I love speed, and I have a high-risk nature. Of course, placing high-potential trades is all about fast decisions and fast trade execution. I am very passionate about the financial markets and believe them to be the most exciting place on earth. With that said, I must say trading is probably one of the unhealthiest occupations I know of. Sitting in one chair all day, I sometimes become so focused I forget to eat, drink, and even breathe. In addition, focusing on multiple flashing computer screens for hours at a time takes a toll on one's eyes, and certainly "traders' spread" can become a problem. It is a real challenge for most of us who immerse ourselves in the markets to maintain a healthy mental, emotional, and physical balance in our lives.
What personal qualities helped you to become a trader?	My high tolerance for risk — which I did not know I had when I started trading — was at first a curse. Now that I have learned to tame and discipline that trait, however, I believe it has become a blessing. I am also a card-carrying member of the Perfectionists Club. That trait can also be a nuisance to traders (and most traders are A-type, perfectionist personalities). Perfectionists have a habit of "watching themselves" trade, then criticizing every move. That can lead to losses and result in overtrading in an attempt to recoup those losses.

SUCCESS STORY: TONI TURNER	
	If you are a perfectionist, stop beating yourself up — it colors your perception of the market and causes drawdowns. Instead, turn your perfectionism to your advantage by using it to plan and execute your trades with precision.
What advice would you give potential traders?	Before you start trading, study the markets and how they work. At a minimum, learn the basics of fundamental and technical analysis.
	Then, decide on your goals. What do you want from trading? Income? To build wealth? To provide a profitable retirement occupation?
	How much time can you devote to it?
	Develop a business plan. Trading incurs expenses, just like every other business.
	Do some personal introspection — can you tolerate risk and the fact that sometimes you will lose money?
	Create objectives — not monetary objectives at first — but process-oriented objectives (such as: "This week I will study interrelationships between 60-minute, daily, and weekly charts").
	Learn risk-reward analysis, and use it to plan your trades. Then trade your plan with discipline.
	My list of advice to potential traders can go on for many pages. At the end of the day, remember that trading is not a destination; it is a journey. I still learn from every trade I make. The day I stop learning will be the day I stop trading.
When did you know that you would be successful?	I knew I would be successful when my bottom line started rising — consistently — over a period of months. I had finally learned to trade minus the emotions that plague most traders — greed and fear. That is probably the most difficult lesson to learn for traders: to learn to trade without emotions that cause bad decisions.
	Of course, as humans, we are wired to feel something. I strive to trade each day with a calm confidence that comes from

SUCCESS STORY: TONI TURNER	
	applying a plan to each trade and the discipline and experience to execute according to that plan.
Which stock indicator do you pay the most attention to?	I use a variety of indicators because I teach trading, and I want to be able to explain how the most popular indicators act in different times and in different situations. They all have their quirks, benefits, and drawbacks. I suppose my favorite chart indicators are candle technology, moving averages, MACD (moving average convergence divergence indicator), Directional Indicators (+ and -DI and ADX), Stochastics, and on-balance volume. Actually, studying volume momentum and all of its nuances and then analyzing it in correlation with price momentum has proven a very worthwhile project.

TRADING TACTICS

If the foregoing has not frightened you off by now, then here are a few pointers that are particularly applicable to the fast pace of day trading. You should not forget all the previous discussions on charting, as you will find that the patterns and signals are scalable, that is, if a pattern will work over a period of days, weeks or months, it is equally valid over a period of minutes.

We have already mentioned the practice of scalping. This is the process of drawing a profit from small market fluctuations. Trading is basically a zero-sum game between traders, but this is never more true than in the practice of scalping, where you are head-to-head with other traders, each of you trying to outwit the other. This is a high-risk activity, as you need to trade in large amounts to cover the slippage, and you can be caught out by a sliding price when other traders take their profit. Hanging on in the hopes of a recovery may not be a good plan. You need to take your loss by selling at market, as a conditional trade may not save you. If you want to scalp, you need to be buying lots of 1,000 shares, and you will make cents on each share.

Other day trading tactics are more in line with the short-term principles expounded on previously. Again, the charts are scalable. If you identify a trend in the five-minute chart, it is as playable as one in the daily chart, except you must expect that the trend will go through its cycle more quickly. If you are playing a trend, you may not need to buy 1,000 shares to cover your slippage, but you still need to be thinking in large numbers and determining your expected profit for your exit point.

TIMING IS EVERYTHING

When you start looking into day trading, you may need to spend a day or two just looking at your favorite stocks' movements to understand the rhythm of the day. There are some distinct characteristics during the day, and you need to understand these so that you will not be caught out.

First, when the market opens, you get all the activity that has been ordered overnight hitting the market. You can easily see a jump in price when the stock opens because of the buying pressure, which will often reverse after the trades have cleared.

The next period that causes noticeable effects is the lunchtime. The activity level may slow, and there may be some closing out of earlier moves, because the traders will not be at their screens if they take a lunch. As there is not so much volume, you may find that the prices vary more widely, and this can be a time to watch out, as stocks may not move as planned.

By mid-afternoon, you should see some clarity in the underlying movement, as the buyers and sellers come to a balance point and agreement on the value for the day. However, within the last hour of trading, you will find another price effect, as the traders get out of their positions so that they do not have to hold them overnight. There may a big effect from the institutional traders, who will sort out their positions in this time.

SUCCESS BULLETS

- You need Level II access to the markets to keep up with the pace of day trading.

- Federal regulations control your actions and account size when you are categorized as a pattern day trader, which depends on how many trades you make.

- You will need to buy in lots of 1,000 shares to make much money out of the cents per share that you can win on day trading.

- Many day traders lose money for the first six months while learning.

- You do not need to hold positions all the time, if there is no money to be made.

- As a novice, you may hesitate and miss opportunities, but you should not try to catch up with trends.

- Scalping is a high-risk activity that more than any other trading brings you into direct competition with other traders.

- You should study the movements of stocks during the day to see the effects of different time periods.

WORDS TO KNOW

Flat, pattern day trading

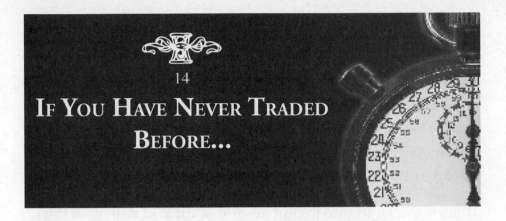

14
IF YOU HAVE NEVER TRADED BEFORE...

You want to start trading, and now you need the specifics of what to do. As you have read this book so far, you have a good idea of all the things that are necessary, but you need to put them together to make a good start.

The first thing to note is that you need to set up your trading as a business. This way, you can maximize your tax benefits and claim your computer setup and Internet connection as business expenses. Keep a clear record of all your expenditures for tax time. Because you may be working from home, you can also claim portions of your bills as expenses. Note that tax matters are different if you qualify as a pattern day trader. Although this means that you have a minimum account size and more possibility of falling foul of the regulations, if you maintain your number of trades to be considered a pattern day trader you do get additional tax benefits. Bear in mind that trading gains are short-term capital gains, being held for less than one year and are taxed at a higher level than long-term capital gains, so you may need all the help you can get.

If you do not yet have your computer, you may want to

consider buying one that is capable of being upgraded to an integrated trading platform of your choice.

At this stage, for a new trader, you may not need to buy the platform, as you can just use your browser while you learn the ropes. You will also need to arrange your Internet connection and get this up and running before you progress to any other items.

Before you rush into losing money — for you will have losing trades, particularly as you are learning — you would be well advised to practice with some "paper trading." Opinions vary on how effective "paper trading," or pretending to trade by writing down your intended moves, can be, as you are not experiencing the real emotional impact of using and losing your money. However, going through the process of identifying stocks from your criteria and deciding what percentage of your trading account to place in them and where to set your stops, encourages you to think trades through and eases the transition when you start in earnest. It is then up to your will power as to whether you can trade in a manner similar to the paper trades.

If you want to rely on the broker for your charts, you need to do research on what the different brokers have available before deciding which one to use. If you are serious about trading as a business, consider purchasing charting software, in which case you would be more interested in your broker's charges and efficiency.

Bill Poulos, in the accompanying Case Study, expresses his thoughts about accepting the inevitability of losing trades and the need for good charting software.

SUCCESS STORY: BILL POULOS

Bill Poulos has been trading the markets since 1974. He is a retired automotive executive who holds a bachelor's degree in industrial engineering and a master's degree in business administration, with a major in finance.

During his more than 30 years of trading experience, Bill has developed dozens of trading systems and methods. In 2001, he formed Profits Run, Inc. to impart his trading experience and wisdom to others so they could short-cut their learning curve and ultimately potentially skyrocket their earnings in the markets.

Bill now has thousands of students all around the world, from all walks of life and at all experience levels. He prides himself on providing honest and realistic trading education and is known for the continuous and ongoing support and follow-up he offers his students. Visit his Web site **www.profitsrun.com** for more details.

What types of trading are you involved with?	Swing trading stocks (and options) with minimum 500,000 daily volume as well as swing trading the major Forex pairs.
How did you start trading?	While attending college majoring in engineering, I always had a fascination about how the markets worked and that there must be some logical order that could be identified and taken advantage of. Not unlike solving an engineering challenge.
What were your main concerns when starting trading?	Finding an approach that would never lose and having enough money to start trading. Finding an approach where I could jump in with a small account and begin making money immediately, instead of being deliberate about mastering a good method by paper trading that I would then own for life and be able to trade when the money became available down the road. Also, how to fit trading into an already full-time work schedule, raising a family, and so on.
How soon did you see a steady flow of income?	Not until years later.
What are your likes and dislikes about trading?	I like the challenge of being able to develop an edge that will give me an advantage trading the markets. I did not like the long hours it took me to figure out how to do that.
What personal qualities helped you to become a trader?	Tenacity, discipline, controlling emotions.

SUCCESS STORY: BILL POULOS	
What is the biggest challenge you have faced in trading?	To stop listening to the so-called experts who are well intended but do not enable one to make money consistently with their advice. To realize that there is no holy grail of trading, I wasted a lot of time with my engineer's mentality thinking I could develop methods that would never lose. Once I finally realized that was not possible, nor was it necessary to succeed, that is when I started to make real progress.
What advice would you give potential traders?	First, realize that there is no holy grail of trading. Trading is about gaining an edge in the market that will allow you to win over a series of trades, but there will be losing trades along the way. Second, do not trade without a good method that includes specific setup conditions, entry rules, and exit rules. Third, use good money-management principles. Without this a trader will lose even with a good method. Fourth, if possible, find a mentor who can guide the beginner to becoming a success. Many beginning traders do none of the above, and as a consequence, lose their money, jump from one "holy grail" method (promising the moon) to the next, and just keep on losing, and finally give up all together. This is a very common problem among beginning traders, where they want to jump in with a small account, after studying a good method for a couple of weeks and are then disappointed because they had a losing trade or two or three. Most of them lose because they do not apply the method properly to begin with and they lose because they over trade, or their position size is out of line with account size. Instead the beginner should find a good method and then take the time, as long as it takes, to master the method by paper trading, which includes the experience of how the markets work, and gain a feel for the market action anchored around whatever trading method they are following. Then when the money comes down the road they will be ready to trade with a good method that they then own for life.
What qualities do you think are important in a would-be trader?	Take personal responsibility for what happens to them, tenacity, discipline, realistic expectations, determination to be successful no matter what.

SUCCESS STORY: BILL POULOS	
When did you know that you would be successful?	When I realized there was no holy grail of trading and that was not necessary to do well.
Describe your typical day.	Each morning I adjust the exit orders on any open positions according to my exit strategy. Then I run my daily scans according to my method's search criteria that will identify trade candidates that are likely to meet my method's setup conditions. I then evaluate those candidates and decide which I will place entry orders for that day, if any. And that is it. The whole process takes 20 minutes, and then I am done for the day. No need to watch the market intraday.
What is the biggest trading mistake you ever made?	Not using stops and carrying position sizes that were far too big for my account size.
Which stock indicator do you pay the most attention to?	There are over a hundred technical and fundamental indicators. All of them have some merit. The key is to select a few, no more than a handful, that are then applied in an uncommon way to develop a superior trading method. There is no magic in the indicators; it is how you apply them that makes the difference.
Describe your setup of computer, software, and Internet connection.	Very simple: high-speed Internet, good charting software, and good desktop computer. An important point here is that many beginning traders try to get by with substandard charting software and think that they are going to compete with other traders with superior charting software. It just is not going to happen. And this is not necessary, because there are so many good charting software packages to choose from that are reasonably priced.

If you are not using your broker's charts, you will need to buy some charting software and subscribe to a data feed at this stage. Although these items do have to talk intimately with each other, and you should check for compatibility, most common software packages can handle any of the popular feeds. An online search will identify the different software packages available — the standards include MetaStock and TradeStation, and other packages are available, such as AmiBroker, which are slightly cheaper. It is hard to find any charting software worthy of the name that will not do everything that you want of it, but look also for the add-ons, which include pre-programmed search criteria and data manipulation, which can add significantly to the cost but are useful. Again, at the learning stage, you may not bother with the add-ons while you are getting comfortable with the basics, but it is good to know what is available.

Now you can get down to some real analysis and start figuring what indicators you want to try trading with. You are well advised to always use at least two independent indicators to denote your trading condition, even if the second is only for confirmation and not a primary signal, and you must also have in your plan what to do when they do not agree. You may spend a significant amount of time and effort in developing your trading system at this stage, and you are laying the groundwork for your future career, so it is time well spent.

When you consider your system, you will also need to decide what your financial resources are for trading — remembering that this is money that you should be prepared to say goodbye to without jeopardizing your life or life style. More on this later in the chapter, but you will need to think about your maximum losses and gains and how large they are in comparison to the total amount that you are trading with. If you wipe out a large section of your trading funds, it can take a long time to recover, if ever. We would suggest risking losing say 2 percent of your fund. This does not mean that you only put 2 percent of your account into a trade, far from it. It would take a long time to amass any profit on that basis. No, it means that your immediate stop-loss price on taking on the stock would permit you to lose only 2 percent maximum of your total trading capital. As your stop-loss percentage will be set from the trading method that you adopt, this will govern the maximum that you should put into that particular stock. In any case, you would be unwise to trade with more than 25 percent of your account in any particular stock.

MAKING YOUR ENTRANCE

Some traders set great store on finding the perfect time to enter a trade. You may find in the more advanced textbooks whole chapters written about "setups." A setup is, quite simply, a set of conditions in a stock that will give you a reason to enter or buy the stock.

There are different schools of thought on this particular topic. You may see that the professional traders who contributed to the case studies in this book emphasize simplicity and discipline as the main factors in their work. That is easy for them to say, as, after years of trading, they may well recognize setups, in the context of the right time to get into a promising stock, without too much formality in the process. The range of views is clear from the following expert views.

David Jenyns, in his *Ultimate Trading Systems* e-book, available at **ultimate-trading-systems.com**, asserts that the entry point contributes only 10 percent to the profits and dismisses the belief of many beginning traders that there is a holy grail to get you into winning trades. He also quotes in his book from a work by Van K. Tharp which shows that in 10 different markets a random choice of entry still made money, primarily, it seems, because of a close stop position, so that any unfavorably moving stocks were quickly sold off.

A second view is given by Toni Turner in her book *Short-Term Trading in the New Stock Market*. She advises, particularly for the newcomer, "to become a specialist in one or two setups" and suggests that to try more may lead to mastering none.

Contrast this to the position of Alan S. Farley, outlined in the influential work *The Master Swing Trader*. He details in chapter after chapter setups with esoteric names that would seem to identify optimal opportunities for market entry. This book emphasizes the concept of pattern recognition via intuition and visualization in its discussion of successful trading and is more directed toward discretionary systems, where the experienced trader exercises choice. This is not for the fainthearted, or, indeed, the inexperienced.

It does not hurt to become familiar with some common setups. The type of trading system you use will influence how useful it will be to your trading, and increasing your knowledge will help your trading career. However you get there, you will identify the stock you want to buy and assess the initial stop position. This will depend on your trading method, but may be, for example, just below the support price in case you get a downside breakout.

A quick calculation later, and you will know how much you can afford to risk. You do not plan to lose, but you should plan to not lose more than 1 percent to 2 percent of your money on any one trade. You may not even want to go in for that much when starting to trade, but you have to balance your risk with the potential gain and realize that you must cover your trading costs and plan for a decent profit. You may well adjust your maximum on the strength of the signal that you just read, putting in more if you think that the win is likely — however, at this stage, you may not possess much discernment of that quality. As you develop this sense, bear in mind that you can enter or exit a position in stages. Even though this would attract more commission costs, you may find situations where the price breakaway that you anticipated is so strong that you wish you would put more money in, for example, and you could enter a further amount, maybe resetting your stop-loss on the original trade at the same time and thus fixing those profits so that you still do not risk losing more than 2 percent on the trade.

MANAGING THE RIDE

Next you have your order in place, and you have covered any potential losses with a stop-loss order. Depending what sort of trading you are doing, you are either watching the screen like a hawk or waiting for something to happen sometime. It would be usual to have, say, up to five positions open at once without being stretched about keeping an eye on them. If you have the time, start working on your next trading idea, as you will not achieve much by sitting around. By putting your maximum loss at 1 percent for any trade, you are more able to detach yourself from the outcome and try to trade on facts, not feelings.

Now is the time for which you have saved all your Zen-like moments. You need to detach and be an observer of your trades. You need not be motionless if something is to be done according to your system's trading rules. It will go a whole lot more smoothly if you do not try adjusting your plan on the fly on the basis of a gut feeling. It is natural to believe that the trades you have made are due to come about after all the effort that you have put in to developing your system. The simple fact is that the market will do what it wants, without reference to your justification of the expectation of a rise. Human nature makes you want to be proven right, and this can lead to breaches in discipline and resetting stops, which have been shown to be detrimental in practice.

If your stocks are rising as you foresaw, then good; you may wish to raise your stop-loss order level to preserve some of your profits. If your stocks are falling in a way you did not predict and you get stopped out of the stock by your stop-loss order, then good, too; this is precisely what is meant to happen to preserve your capital and your sanity.

MAKING YOUR EXIT

Of course, you have planned your exits from each of the positions that you are in, and you did so as part of your system on selecting the stocks. You have multiple exits, as you have one exit if the price drops, your stop-loss; and another exit, typically a trailing stop, if things go as planned. Iron will is the key to making the correct play. Emotions can affect your decisions and actions, and this would be perfectly natural — after all, that is real money that you have at stake. You must remember to "let your profits run and cut your losses short," which runs counter to many of your feelings.

If the price immediately drops, you may feel that you are still right, that it is a temporary fluctuation, and if anything, it represents an opportunity to buy more of this stock at a lower price and make more profit when it turns. If instead the stock rises as you hoped, you may be tempted to sell to make real the gain and count a win for your system. You can see how both these instincts act to sabotage your goal. You can get around this by ensuring that your exit rules are as clearly written down as your entrance rules. Look back at the Stopping Out section in Chapter 12 if you need a refresher on the ways that you may determine that it is worth selling up, but above all, make sure that you do have a stop in place on every trade.

A word about setting the stops with the broker. This may be the best you can do, particularly if you may be inclined to be distracted by family, telephone calls, and honey-do lists. However, there is a school of thought that you should never set the stops for automatic selling at a certain point. This may depend on whether you intend to trade live or are just interested in maintaining day to day or weekly trades. The argument is, first, that the intraday prices may fluctuate enough to trigger the selling, when the real trend, as evidenced by closing prices, is still on the rise.

The second problem is that the order is "out there," and some people are suspicious enough to think that this alone may cause some crafty trader shenanigans. Certainly, you may want to use slightly odd values for your stops — if the point is 25 percent, for example, perhaps you want 24 percent. This is because experienced traders will guess the more obvious points and try to hit them to cause moves that they want. Or, others will set the 25 percent as a standard, so there will be many traders trying to sell if the stock reaches that level; thus, because of the supply, you will not actually get out at 25 percent but perhaps 30 percent. A stop-loss order becomes a market order when the level is reached, so you will get what the market will give you when all those shares are offered for sale. The other side is that, if you do not have an automatic sell order in place, you may use discretion in exiting the stock, and this upsets a well-designed system's performance; that is, you are likely to be trading with emotion again.

Finally, you should start keeping a trading diary/notebook. This is for several good reasons. First, you need to have accurate records for tax time. You can use the back of your trading diary to make a note of incidental expenses, to keep all the information in one place. If there are any tax issues when you submit your return, you will be able to impress any auditor that you are not just guessing at the figures.

Second, you need to review your trades, both winning and losing, at frequent intervals, and see if you think that an adjustment in your trading system would be worth trying. Your system should evolve over time, and it can do this only if you make a point of checking where it is working and where it seems to let you down. Backtest any proposed changes to build your confidence in them, and then let them loose on your account.

Third, for the longer view, you want to have access to the

information that you can use to assess how you are doing. From time to time you need to gather together your data and look at your performance. You need to figure out your percentage of winning trades and the average size of winners compared to losers — if you are cutting your losses short and letting your winners run. This sort of information will enable you to take a view of your performance as a trader and figure out any weak points that need to be worked on.

SUCCESS BULLETS

- Treat trading as a business from the start.

- Use paper trading to develop your ability to follow your plan without bringing emotion into it.

- Research any appealing suggestions from Chapter 12 to decide on your trading system.

- Commit sufficient resources to your trading, but ensure that you do not put yourself in the position of losing more than 1 percent to 2 percent per trade or put more than 25 percent of your account in any one trade.

- Study setups to increase your familiarity with the charts.

- Aim to have five to ten trades active at any one time but only if you have suitable stocks to trade in.

- Consider odd values for stop-losses to prevent experienced market traders from second-guessing your moves.

Quotes

Market Summary

October 2, 2002

Dow Jones Industrial Average

		7,950
		7,920
		7,890
		7,860
		7,830
11	1	3	7,800

▼ DJIA		7,904.45	-34.34
▼ NASDAQ		1,212.54	-1.18
▼ S&P 500		845.84	-2.07

As of 12:09 PM ET
© BigCharts.com

3rd Party Research

Disclosure

15

IN THE END — SELF CARE

Few things in life cause more stress than money issues — love, maybe, although even that is open to debate. Although you will make some money when you are trading if you follow this book's advice, you are also sure to lose some. This is different from the normal work environment, where you just do the hours and it miraculously transforms into cash later. Working under this sort of pressure is certain to result in a different perspective and touch on feelings that you may not have known you possessed.

Particularly for those who choose to trade during the day, but also for anyone involved in trading with its inevitable losses as well as gains, you need to be aware of and considerate toward yourself and those around you. Realize that you may become somewhat disconnected with your true self that you and others are used to. Work to take a larger view of your life and to reinforce the balance that you need for your own health and for sanity.

THE IMPORTANCE OF YOUR MIND-SET

In his book *Trade Your Way to Financial Freedom*, Dr. Van Tharp talks about the role of psychology in trading. He even puts a percentage on it, with 10 percent of trading being the system, 30 percent money management, and 60 percent being the trader's psychology. In other words, the trader's psychology has more to do with his success than the other factors combined.

Most books on trading emphasize that, without control of your emotions, you are doomed to fail at trading. It is in the nature of people to think that we can control ourselves, so you may think that you are impervious to this weakness. However, when you stop and consider that the failed traders have read the same books and still failed, perhaps you have a reason to hesitate in your self-assurance. Just as you intend to work at learning trading, you need to work at care of yourself, which will give you the strength to carry it through.

Self-care, if you are to become a habitual and successful trader, starts with the psychology of the trade — if it stresses you out too much each time you trade, then you will not last. You need to be aware of and work on your mind-set, just as all successful traders have. The power of positive thinking is a well-worn expression, but it is a fact that you need to tap into an inner mental power and ensure that your attitude is positive and clear. The way you choose to trade is key to enabling this.

At the start of this journey, fear and greed dominating the whole trading scene was discussed. To this add pride, hope, denial, disbelief, and other negative emotions. The first point to overcome — or reduce to a realistic size — those emotions, is to be sure in your own mind that the amount you are trading with may be chalked up to experience with no deeper impact if things do not work out. Thus, you can get some detachment from the cash.

The second point is that you must have a plan, or system, in which you have confidence, and then you can follow the plan without question as the market unfolds. This in itself can reduce stress. This comes from extensive backtesting of your system, and you certainly need to have an attitude that accepts that losses are frequent, and it is not a particular attack on your manhood (or womanhood) or your system. Losers are just the nature of the market, which is substantially larger than you or I.

Know that your confidence in your system will be questioned by the market. If you do stray from your discipline, it may just be that time that the market responds and rewards you, and you will have a subconscious reaction that you can outthink the system. You may also trade your system with focused commitment only to find that the market is contrary, and this will also be logged in your subconscious as a fault with your system. Every trader has felt these emotions — arguably, to ignore them is one of the major lessons that is often not truly learned until you have traded for some time.

THE IMPORTANCE OF PHYSICAL CARE

Taking the previous words to heart will ensure that you are as psychologically prepared for your trading as possible; however, for balance, self-care also covers your physical state, which in turn also affects your mind-set directly. Bear in mind that you may be spending significant time hunched over a computer, staring at a screen. This is not the recommended way to stay fit. When you start your trading may be the ideal time to start the workout program that you keep promising yourself. Exercise can release endorphins that will bring about a natural good feeling, assisting your well-being and helping in your trading success.

This is not a keep-fit book; however, here are some words of advice about your physical well-being. First, whatever form it takes, make sure that you establish a routine for your exercise. This is a lifetime commitment and should be selected to be enjoyable and sustainable. Second, do not overdo it, especially at first, as you will not keep it up, and you can risk injury or worse. Also, if you think that you need to, do see your doctor for a checkup before undertaking anything strenuous.

One of the simplest and most enjoyable ways of getting a basic level of exercise is also in keeping with Doug & Sherri Brown's dedication to Bear, at the beginning of this book. Yes, get a dog or two from a rescue organization, and walk them at least once and preferably twice a day. This is exercise that is hard to skip, as you see the expectation and joy in your dog's face at walk time. A real and unshakable commitment to exercise every day is one of the hardest things to make, and here is the ideal no-hassle solution. You get many incidental benefits from caring for an animal, and dogs, particularly rescue dogs, are always appreciative of your attention. It will give you a tremendous feeling of well-being to know that you have saved an animal and friend from possible death. If you are an early riser and live in the country, you may also get a spiritual uplift from an early morning walk with your dog.

You should also plan to build up from this basic level of movement with cardio activity, stuff that does get your heart beating faster and even make you sweat, by taking on a more focused type of training perhaps three or four times a week. The trader working at home should get some exercise apparatus. When you are employed and go to work each day, it is nothing to drop in to a gym you are passing by on the way home or to go out to the health club at lunch break. When you are working from home, it is easy to put off driving somewhere for the same exercise — it may be raining or snowing, or you just do not feel like leaving your cozy (or air-conditioned) home. The answer is to bring the machine to you. Whether it is a treadmill, stair climber, or multi-gym is not as important as the principle of getting and using something regularly.

The alternative and compelling way to exercise is to join a sports club, to play tennis or racquetball, for example, and make sure that you sign up for the club competitions. Again, you will have difficulty in avoiding the exercise, as you are committed to other people, and this can be a key factor in keeping to your drill. You will need all the will power you can muster to work efficiently at your trading, and you do not need to be finding more inner strength to keep up your exercise program, so make it easy on yourself and make commitments that you have to keep.

While talking about the physical side, we should mention nutrition and eating properly. This is more important than you may realize if you intend to be day trading, as this activity relies on you being awake and alert while in a position. Unfortunately, much of the more popular food has the opposite effect.

Eat properly — again, there are countless books available covering this topic, and you should appreciate that it is all part of self-care. The situation of sitting at a desk all day, if that is the way that you implement your trading, is inviting mindless nibbling on snacks that are high in fat, tasty, and bad for you. Consider instead crunching on carrots or other more healthy alternatives. You can make lunch before you start, a healthy sandwich of some sort, which will save you from leaving your desk and allow you to keep in touch with the market.

THE IMPORTANCE OF SPIRITUAL LIFE

Now, this is not a self-improvement book, at least not in the normal sense of the words, but having covered the mind and the body, it would be remiss not to mention the care of the spiritual side. Particularly as your trading life is going to be so focused on the material world, you need to nurture your spirit. This is a topic where the advice must be integrated into your personal belief system. Many people, while they may have shunned a childhood and childish image of God, have a sense of a greater power at work in the universe and in their lives. Perhaps as simple as "it was meant to be," this association and relationship outside of our personal physical boundaries is an essential part of who we are as human beings.

If you have an organized faith or religion that involves services or meetings, I would encourage you to take up regular attendance and to taking your part in any aid or outreach programs that they run. You will find that even tiring work in a good cause, disconnected from the day-to-day practice of trading, can be incredibly refreshing. To further refresh your spirit daily, you need to contact that higher power by whatever means is in your spiritual vocabulary. This may involve prayer, meditation, yoga, or simple reflection. Take time to ground yourself every day. It can help to have some quiet introspection at dawn. I recommend some of the less esoteric writings of Stuart Wilde, who in his *Infinite Self* work suggests that we personify our tribal instincts and the things that limit us, which separate us from our higher being, as the "ego," and in doing so reduce them to a size that we can deal with, allowing our underlying infinite being to have its voice in our lives.

Some other suggested sources of guidance in life balance, who are more mainline than Stuart, are Dr. Deepak Chopra and Dr. Wayne Dyer, both of whom have published many works. I have and recommend their books and tapes. In spiritual matters, more than any other aspect, the path you take is intensely personal, and you need to explore it for yourself.

Above all, what I am advocating is conscious balance in your life. Take time to view your world from 30,000 feet and determine where you may need to redirect your efforts to become more in tune with yourself and the universe. In this way, you will find that trading, and everything else you attempt, will take a natural path that leads you on to greater fulfillment and success.

SUCCESS BULLETS

- Learn to master your psychology, knowing that this is crucial to trading success.

- Do not neglect your physical well-being because of the intensity of the trading world.

- Nurture your spirit to become more balanced in your life.

SUMMARY

This book has encapsulated the knowledge that you will need to decide if short-term trading is for you and to know how to start trading. Professional traders emphasize the need for continual education, and, although this may be the first, it will not be the last book that you study if you become an active trader.

Success in trading seems to come from two distinct sources. First, you have to develop a trading plan that you can believe in and that suits your life style and capabilities. If you do not, all indications are that you will certainly fail to make money, as most traders do. Second, you have to develop the mind-set that allows you to follow your trading plan without trying to second-guess it, unless, of course, you are a certified psychic; otherwise again you will join the ranks of the majority of would-be traders who do not make money.

The success stories included show that it is quite possible to make a living from trading, and that, although it is not an easy task, it is rewarding for those to whom it appeals. It offers a unique life style, which at its best can liberate you to make money from anywhere in the world at any time.

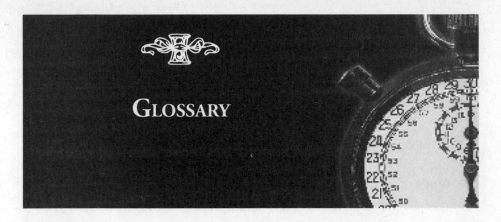

Glossary

Amex: The American Stock Exchange, which trades stocks too small for the NYSE.

Ask: The price at which a stock is for sale from the dealers.

Average Directional Movement Index (ADX): An indicator that shows the strength of a price movement.

Bar Chart: A chart showing the price of a security against time. The price is indicated by a vertical bar, which shows the range in price for the period, often one day. Horizontal lines on each side show the opening and closing prices for the period.

Bears: Traders and investors who believe that the prices are too high and reduce the values.

Bid: The price that a stock can be sold to the market dealers.

Bollinger Bands: An indicator that is based on a moving average, with the bands spaced at a distance of two standard deviations each side. Indicates volatility.

Bond: A loan to a company or government that will be repaid in preference to shares.

Breakout: A price movement that deviates from the expected price range, either above or below.

Broker: A dealer in stocks or other securities.

Browser-Based: Refers to a charting method that uses a regular Internet browser rather than a custom display.

Bulls: Traders and investors who support an increase in stock prices.

Buy-Side Analyst: An analyst of the market who works for an institution to advise on its investments.

Buy-To-Cover: Buying shares to cover, or hold, a shortage of shares for which an option has been sold.

Call: A type of option, a call is a right to buy a stock at a set price up until a certain date.

Call Away: When shorting a stock, the broker may occasionally call away the shares that were borrowed, resulting in an immediate purchase to cover them.

Candlestick Chart: A form of price chart derived from the same data as the bar chart but which shows more clearly the values and direction of price in a day or other period.

CFD: Contract for difference, this is similar to options in shares, indices and commodities.

Channel: Two lines drawn parallel to the trendline, above and below, which represent the maximum expected price variation.

Consolidation: A stock undergoes a period of consolidation when, in a trend, it pauses and trades at the same value for a time before continuing the trend.

Covered Call: In options trading, when you sell a call, you are said to cover it if you also buy the shares for which you may be called.

Cup-With-Handle: A price pattern that may indicate the start of an uptrend.

Day Trader, Day Trading: Day trading refers to trading for the shortest periods, with all trades settled at the end of each day.

Direct-Access Broker: This is a broker who is able to give the trader access to the market directly.

Direct-Access Platform: The means by which you access the market, a computer and software combination.

Discount Broker: A broker who provides a share buying and selling service at a lower price than a full-service broker but without advice and other features.

Dividend: Some companies make a dividend payment to the shareholder at intervals, which encourages the purchase of their shares and increases their value.

Doji: A single shape on the candlestick chart, where the body of the candle is only a line and has no length.

Double-Bottom: A pattern on a price chart that may indicate a change to an uptrend.

Downtrend: A price that is reducing over time.

Dragonfly Doji: A special form of doji that has no upper shadow.

Engulfing Pattern: A pair of opposite-colored adjacent candlesticks, where the later one is larger above and below the first one, engulfing it.

Equities: Another word for stocks.

ETF: Exchange-traded fund; this is a basket of shares in a particular market.

Exercise: In this context, to exercise an option is to take it up.

Exit Point: The value at which you have decided that you will sell a stock and exit the trade.

Fibonacci: An Italian mathematician, Leonardo of Pisa; a number sequence in which the sum of two consecutive numbers equals the next number.

Fill: The price at which your order to buy or sell shares is completed is called the fill.

Flag: A pattern that can be drawn on a price chart, a period of consolidation.

Flat: A day trader is said to be flat when he or she sells out positions every day.

Forex: Short for Foreign Exchange, this is the market for buying currencies.

Free Riding: Selling a stock before you have paid for it, during the three-day payment settlement period.

Full-Service Broker: A dealer in stocks and shares who will offer advice and assist in trading.

Fundamental Analysis: Analyzing the financial state of a company from basic data, such as the financial reports, revenues, capital investment, and growth.

Futures: A contract to buy or sell an agreed amount of a commodity at a set price at a set time in the future.

Gravestone Doji: A special form of doji that has no lower shadow.

Gross Domestic Product: The value of goods and services produced in the United States in a period.

Hammer: A candlestick shape that looks like a hammer; it has no upper shadow and a short body.

Head-And-Shoulders: A charting pattern that often signals the end of a trend.

Indicators: Tools for technical analysis of stock charts, indicators are developed from data to signal potential price movements.

Integrated Trading Platform: A computer and software combination that gives easy access to trades.

Intraday: Intraday data is price movement occurring during the day and is essential to the day trader.

Level I/II: Levels of detail in share trading data. Level I is the basic bid/ask price and other information available at a broker or financial Web site; Level II adds more details, is constantly updated, and shows individual trading action. It is useful for day trading but not necessary for short-term trading.

Leverage: Multiplies the effective amount invested, as in using options, so that a small increase in share price would make a much larger return.

Limit Order: An order to buy or sell shares that sets a maximum price you will pay, or a minimum you will sell at, and is not filled unless the limit is reached.

Line Chart: A basic chart of price change over time, with a line drawn through the price point for each time period.

Liquidity: A stock has good liquidity if there is much trading in that stock, and it is therefore easy to buy and sell without distorting the market price.

Long: To be long is to buy a stock or financial instrument.

Margin: A margin is a facility given to traders to borrow from the broker, up to the amount deposited.

Margin Call: When you have used a margin facility, you are subject to a margin call, which requires you to pay back the borrowed money if you suffer losses and no longer comply with minimum funding requirements.

Market Makers: These people trade on behalf of clients and maintain liquidity in the market for the NASDAQ.

Market Order: An order to your broker to buy or sell shares at the best price obtainable in the market at the time.

Momentum Indicator: An indicator that gives a measure of the increase or decrease in momentum of a stock price movement.

Momentum Trading: Buying a stock that is rising in price, on the basis that it will keep on rising.

Moving Average: A line indicator plotted on a price chart, this is a family of values. A moving average is plotted from the average price value for the previous number of days, computed day by day, and the number of days can be varied as needed.

Moving Average Convergence/Divergence (MACD): An indicator based on moving average computations.

NASDAQ: National Association of Securities Dealers Automated Quotations, an electronic stock market, mainly known for trading technology stocks.

NYSE: New York Stock Exchange.

Option Holder: The buyer of an option, giving the opportunity to buy or to sell a certain stock at a set price within a set time.

Option Writer: The person or group selling the option.

Options: An option allows the purchaser to buy a stock at a declared price within a certain time or to sell a stock at a declared price within a certain time. There is no compulsion to go through with the stock transaction, and the option has no value if it is not taken up by the due date.

Order: A command to your broker to deal in shares on your behalf.

Oscillators: Indicators that are designed to show the stock value in relation to its recent trading range.

OTCBB: Over-the-counter or bulletin board, referring to a type of stock that does not qualify to be traded in one of the big markets and thus is more difficult to invest in. Not of interest to the short-term trader, who needs liquidity.

Pattern day trading: If you work at day trading and make a minimum number of trades, you are considered a pattern day trader — this has consequences for your account size and tax position.

P/E: Price versus earnings ratio, a ratio between the stock's current price and the earnings for the past year, which gives a measure of the stock value.

Pennant: A pattern of the price chart that looks like a triangle.

Position Trading: A longer-term trader, the position trader is interested in fundamentals and support for trends that can be followed for days or weeks.

Premium: The amount paid to purchase an option.

Pullback: A pullback is where the price of a stock stops rising or even falls slightly in a long-term uptrend.

Put: The right to sell a stock at a set price, as bought in an option.

Relative Strength Indicator (RSI): A momentum-based indicator that tracks the movement of the prices up and down.

Resistance: A hypothetical line above which a fluctuating stock price will not rise, unless there is a defined change in the perceived value.

Retracement: When a stock price is trending up or down, a retracement is a temporary reversal in the trend.

Reversal Pattern: A pattern on the price chart that suggests that the trend of a stock price is going to reverse.

Scalper, Scalping: Scalping is a method of day trading that relies on making many small and quick gains on regular price fluctuations.

Selling Short: A method to profit from a reduction in the stock price, this involves a technique of selling shares you do not actually own, and buying shares later to replace them.

Sell-Side Analyst: An analyst normally employed by brokers and who may recommend stocks to invest in.

Short: As used in selling short, to be short of a share is, literally, to not own it but owe it to someone – just as you can be short of money to pay a bill, you can be short of a share.

Shippage: Refers to the costs of trading and includes broker commissions and the difference between the bid and ask price.

Specialists: On the NYSE, these people act as auctioneers in any particular stock, bringing together willing buyers and sellers.

Spinning Top: A candlestick pattern where the real body is short, which means that the current move may be running out of steam.

Spread: The difference between bid and ask prices.

Stochastic Oscillator: A momentum-based indicator that includes detailed price data.

Stocks: A stock is a small share in a company. If you owned a sufficient number of them, like Warren Buffett, you could control the company's actions.

Stop: Short for stop order and used interchangeably; setting a stop is placing a stop order.

Stop-Limit Order: Similar to a stop order, but it becomes a limit order when the stop price is reached, providing some protection from a sharp drop and selling at market price.

Stop-Loss Order: This is a stop order, which becomes an order when the price of the stock has dropped to a preset level. The term stop-loss means that it is set at a level that you decide you want to sell at in order to stop any more losses from the falling price

Stop Order: An order that sets a limit to the price of the shares and protects you from too large a drop in value. When it is reached, the order becomes a market order, and the shares are sold at the market price (which may however be lower than the stop order price).

Stopping Out: Reaching a price at which your stocks are sold.

Strike Price: The pre-agreed share price for an option trade.

Support: A hypothetical line below which a fluctuating stock price will not fall, unless there is a defined change in the perceived value.

Swing Trader, Swing Trading: Swing trading is trading for the intermediate term, with positions held from days to weeks. It has some fundamental elements but is based on timing the market with technical analysis and charting.

Technical Analysis: Analyzing the potential short-term movements of a share price by using charts of recent movement and technical indicators and oscillators.

Trailing Stop: A stop order that is self-adjusting as the share price increases. The price on the stop order increases as the maximum share price goes up, but the stop price is never reduced, so it becomes a market sell order if the share price reduces by the amount of offset specified.

Trend: "The trend is your friend." The trend is a strong movement either up or down in the share price. It is often the aim in trading to catch the trend to make a profit.

Triangle: A pattern on the price chart where a triangle can be drawn to embrace the successive price ranges.

Uptick: Important when you want to sell short, an uptick is an upward movement in price.

Uptrend: Share price rising.

Volatility: Extent of price fluctuations.

Volume: The amount of trading that takes place on any stock.

BIBLIOGRAPHY

There are many resources for the prospective trader and many companies who will readily separate you from your money. A Google search for "short-term trading" currently lists more than 4 million results, and "trading" has more than 200 million. You should beware of anyone making extreme claims. The resources mentioned in the text, together with those listed below, I have personal experience of and would recommend.

Secrets of Successful Traders — Experts Reveal Winning Stock Strategies

  Compiled by Equis International

The Master Swing Trader — Tools and Techniques to Profit from Outstanding Short-Term Trading Opportunities

  Alan S. Farley

Ultimate Trading Systems — Your Step-By-Step Roadmap to Trading Success

  David Jenyns

Technical Analysis for Dummies

    Barbara Rockefeller

A Beginner's Guide to Day Trading Online

    Toni Turner

Short-Term Trading in the New Stock Market

    Toni Turner

Trade Your Way to Financial Freedom

    Dr. Van Tharp

AUTHOR DEDICATION & BIOGRAPHY

To my wife Liz, for all that she has done with, for, and alongside me. For accompanying me in life's adventures that took and continue to take us beyond our imagining.

Alan Northcott

Alan Northcott is an author, freelance writer, engineer and farmer, along with other pursuits, and he now lives in the Midwest. Originating from England, he immigrated with his wife to America in 1992. His engineering career spanned more than 30 years, on both sides of the Atlantic, and recent years have found him seeking and living a more diverse and fulfilling life style. You can find out more at **www.alannorthcott.com**, or e-mail him directly at **alannorthcott@msn.com.**

INDEX

C

D

E

THE COMPLETE GUIDE TO INVESTING IN COMMODITY TRADING: HOW TO EARN HIGH RATES OF RETURNS SAFELY

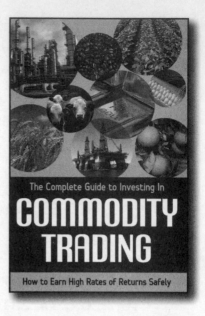

The Complete Guide to Investing In
COMMODITY TRADING
How to Earn High Rates of Returns Safely

Many people have become very rich in the commodity markets. It is one of a few investment areas where an individual with limited capital can make extraordinary profits in a relatively short period of time. Commodities are agreements to buy and sell virtually anything that is harvested — except onions.

Commodity trading can provide you with very high, secure rates of return, in some cases as high as 12%, 18%, 24%, or even 300% or more per year. If performed correctly, commodity trading will far outpace all other investments. The key is to know how to perform this process correctly.

The Complete Guide to Investing in Commodity Trading teaches you what commodity trading and futures are, how to set up your account online, how to choose software to use in trading, how to invest in commodities, evaluate their performance, and handle fees and taxes. This book explores numbers of investing strategies and tactics, charting techniques, and position trading. You will pick up the language of a trader so that you recognize terminology and know how to use leverage, call options, put options, and much more.

ISBN-13: 978-1-60138-003-6
288 Pages • $24.95

THE COMPLETE GUIDE TO INVESTING IN HEDGE FUNDS: HOW TO EARN HIGH RATES OF RETURNS SAFELY

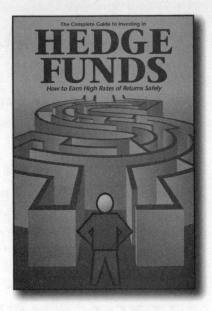

Money managers have traditionally used hedge funds as they would mutual funds: to pool investors' money and place it in financial instruments in an effort to make a high positive return. Hedge funds have typically been available only to the very affluent or to investors with inside contacts, but today that has changed. Almost any investor can now participate in a hedge fund and earn high returns.

Hedge funds can provide you with very high, secure rate of return — 12%, 18%, 24%, or even 300% — per year. If performed correctly, hedge fund trading will far outpace all other investments. This all sounds great, but what is the catch? There really is none, except you must know what you are doing!

The key is learning how to proceed. This book will provide everything you need to know to get started generating high-investment returns with low risk from start to finish. You will find out how to invest in hedge funds, evaluate their performance, and employ investing strategies and tactics, deftly using the latest technology to set up your account online. You will be able to handle fees, taxes, and risks, and you will get little known data to help you double or even triple your investment – all while avoiding the common traps and pitfalls.

ISBN-13: 978-1-60138-000-5
288 Pages • $24.95

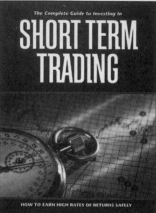